GUNS
101

GUNS 101

A BEGINNER'S GUIDE TO BUYING AND OWNING FIREARMS

David Steier

Skyhorse Publishing

Skyhorse Publishing books may be purchased in bulk at special discounts for sales promotion, corporate gifts, fund-raising, or educational purposes. Special editions can also be created to specifications. For details, contact the Special Sales Department, Skyhorse Publishing, 307 West 36th Street, 11th Floor, New York, NY 10018 or info@skyhorsepublishing.com.

Skyhorse® and Skyhorse Publishing® are registered trademarks of Skyhorse Publishing, Inc.®, a Delaware corporation.

www.skyhorsepublishing.com

10 9 8 7 6

Library of Congress Cataloging-in-Publication Data is available on file.
ISBN: 978-1-61608-287-1

Printed in China

Contents

Acknowledgements

I'D LIKE TO THANK THE FOLLOWING PEOPLE FOR THEIR help and understanding in the preparation of this book. My wife, Carol, and son, Daniel, who put up with me through the process and played editor and "guinea pig" as I bounced ideas and rough drafts off them. Also to my son for his role as "hand model" in several of the shots.

I'd like to also thank the other people who helped me edit or provided photos or guns to be photographed. These include Walt Sippel, Claud Summers, Neil Spruill, Don Smith, and Hugh Howard. Thank you all.

The Ten Commandments of Gun Safety

1. Always keep the muzzle pointed in a safe direction.

2. Guns should be unloaded when not actually in use.

3. Don't rely on your gun's "safety." Treat every gun as if it can fire at any time.

4. Be sure of your target and what's beyond it.

5. Use correct ammunition for your firearm.

6. If your gun fails to fire when the trigger is pulled, *handle with care*. Keep the muzzle pointed in a safe direction and get help.

7. Always wear eye and ear protection when shooting.

8. Be sure the barrel is clear of obstructions before shooting.

9. Don't alter or modify your gun, and *do* have your gun serviced regularly.

10. Learn the mechanical and handling characteristics of the firearm you are using. Do not use any firearm that you have not had adequate instruction in handling.

GUNS
101

Introduction

HI, THANKS FOR TAKING THE FIRST STEP TOWARD OWNING a gun . . . *Finding out something about guns.*

My name is Dave Steier. It might surprise you to know that I was just like *you* about twenty years ago. I didn't come from a "gun/hunting/military" background. While I was interested in guns, I just didn't have the exposure that let me really *learn* about guns. Most of what I knew came from movies and TV. I had heard that "the .44 Magnum is the most powerful handgun ever made and will blow your head clean off." The problem is that most movie and TV people aren't "gun people" either and are frequently wrong.

Eventually, I started reading books and magazines. I then jumped right in and started buying some guns. Then I obtained the training to become an NRA certified range safety officer and certified instructor. As the years rolled by, I became "that guy at the office who's into guns." Friends and coworkers would ask me about guns and learning to shoot. Enough so that I figured it might be helpful to have a short book that they could buy to help give them a foundation that I never had.

Hopefully, I'll be able to steer you away from mistakes I made in choosing firearms to buy, collect, carry, or compete safely.

Overview—Who Should Read This Book?

THIS BOOK IS FOR PEOPLE WHO ARE INTERESTED IN FIRE-arms but don't know anything about them.

This guide will introduce you to the major types of firearms and their uses. The goal is to provide you with enough information to enable you to make a decision. The decision is not only to buy a firearm, but which type of firearm might be right for you.

First, the guide examines the uses of firearms, the most common types of firearms and ammunition, and how firearms work. This will help you understand the jargon that's about to be thrown at you by store salespeople, "helpful friends," and "camo commandos."[1]

Later, the guide will look after the "care and feeding" of your firearm. What to do with it, how to carry it, and how to clean it.

Finally, the guide provides an introduction on where you can shoot your gun and different types of competitions in which you can participate.

---

1 "Camo commandos" are the people who hang out at gun stores, not buying anything and making a general nuisance of themselves. They can be distinguished by inserting themselves in your conversation with the knowledgeable clerks behind the counter (who are just trying to do their job, which is finding *you* the right firearm). Usually the camo commando will try to get you to buy something that *they* think is appropriate, which is seldom what you really want or need.

What This Book Won't Teach You

THIS BOOK IS A SHORT OVERVIEW THAT PREPARES THE reader to start learning more about the world of firearms. This book is not a history of guns (but does have some neat history in its pages). It won't help you to shoot better (unless you take the advice to get lessons). *Finally, this book will not tell you which gun to buy.* There are simply too many to even compile into a book this size, and no single gun is right for everyone. This book *will* prepare you to ask the *right* questions to find the *right* gun.

Guns Are Like Golf Clubs

GOLF CLUBS? I'VE FOUND THAT THERE ARE "GUN PEOPLE" and "antigun people." There is very little middle ground. Some people are predisposed against firearms. Typically, I've found this to be ignorance and fear of something to which they've never been exposed. Often at social gatherings I'm asked, "Why do you need more than one gun?" Typically, the questioner doesn't pause and qualifies their point by saying, "After all, they all just fire a bullet." This is my favorite segue into a conversation about guns. Typically, I retort, "Why does a golfer have more than one club?" Why the question just answers itself. Different clubs are used for different results or terrain (example, you wouldn't use a sand wedge for a long drive off the tee). *Firearms are the same way.* You use different types of firearms for different applications. Consider a revolver. A revolver with an eight-inch barrel is an excellent choice for target shooting or hunting; however, it's awkward to try to fit into a coat pocket for personal defense. Likewise, a two-inch "snub nose" revolver is difficult to shoot accurately at distances over twenty yards.

What Do You *Need* a Gun For?

IN W. E. B. GRIFFIN'S BOOK "*THE CAPTAINS*," A YOUNG OSS agent is asked by his wife, "What do you need a gun for?" The character replies, "You never need a gun, until you need it badly." That line has always stuck with me as an example of not only why to own a gun, but why I made the personal decision to carry a gun. People who are hung up on rhetoric may also add that "Ted Kennedy's car has killed more people than all my guns" in reference to the senator's famous antigun stand. While that statement is true, it's seldom helpful in any kind of debate on gun ownership or rights.

Before you can decide which gun to purchase, you need to determine what activity the gun will be used for. This simple truth should be the main factor for choosing a firearm. Everything else just supports that decision. For example, if you want a firearm for self-defense, you wouldn't want to purchase a rifle in a caliber that is designed to take down elephants.

I've found that the four most stated reasons for owning a gun are (1) personal defense, (2) personal accomplishment/fun/plinking, (3) hunting, and/or (4) collecting. Let's take each of these in turn.

Personal Defense

This is the number one reason most people approach me about buying a firearm, and it's not a bad one. A firearm can be a potent deterrent to violent crime and a lifesaver to someone who has little or no respect for you and your loved ones' lives.

So the key question is, "Can I take somebody else's life?" If the answer is no, then you need to consider other less lethal alternatives such as pepper spray, clubs, knives, martial arts, and such. Many people have ideas that they "will just hold the suspect while waiting for the police" or "shooting to wound." This is an ill-advised strategy. By doing this, you've just created a "trapped animal." And there aren't many trapped animals that wouldn't kill you to escape. So the question remains, "Can you take someone else's life if they are threatening you or your loved ones?" I'll wait.

OK, so you must have answered yes, or are at least keeping an open mind. Owning a gun for personal defense is a great responsibility. Consider the following analogy: Have you ever gone for an extended period (say over two weeks) without driving? Did you notice that your skills had deteriorated when you started driving again? How about parallel parking? Have you tried to parallel park since you took your driver's test? Where I'm going with this is, *owing a firearm is a life choice*. As such, you have a responsibility to practice regularly with your firearm. This means different things to different people. My family and I go through about one thousand rounds of ammunition a month (in a good month). For some people, a quarterly trip to the range is enough. The situation to avoid is buying a firearm and leaving it in a nightstand drawer. That is a recipe for failure when you really need your firearm. Why? Because a gun left on its own without maintenance will collect dust, lubricants will dry out, and will begin to rust. All of that can affect its ability to fire when your life depends on it. Best to take care of it by paying it attention. Going back to the "car analogy," take it out for a spin, but be sure to wash it and get the oil changed regularly.

Personal Accomplishment/Fun/Plinking

This is a catchall section for people who want a gun because they are looking for the recreational aspects that a firearm can provide. Just like most human endeavors, the more you practice, the better you get. It's pretty darn gratifying to be able to hit a target with great regularity and from an increasing distance.

There is also a great thrill of simply shooting at fun, easy-to-destroy targets. In the past, we used to use bottles and Coke cans; however, this creates a huge sharp mess. Better to use soda crackers and suckers that can also feed wildlife and are biodegradable. I can't begin to count the hours I've spent around a lake with a box of .22-caliber bullets and a rifle. *Sigh*, simpler times.

Hunting

Perhaps this section deserves a collective "duh." Lots of people buy a firearm to hunt, and God bless them! Hunting is a necessary part of the ecosystem. There are predators and there are prey. Considering that man has wiped out most of the predators, it's up to us to thin the herd or disease and starvation will set in. I started buying guns in order to hunt. I wanted to "get my own meat." I figured it was very "manly"; however, then I realized that you have to get up *way* before dawn, hike into a "good spot," wait in temperatures that were always either too hot or too cold, and God help you if you actually killed something because then you had to remove its entrails and drag it *out* of the woods. No thanks. I'll just be honest with myself and admit that I collect guns because *i want* to collect guns. I shoot guns because I want to shoot guns.

Collecting

Collectors will collect anything. For some, it's old classic cars, seashells, coins, buttons, why not guns? Truth be known, there are lots of folks who collect guns of certain periods. They try to get every different type of production variant made in order to fill their collection. Go figure.

CHAPTER

I

My *Significant Other* Doesn't Want a Gun in the House

ONE OF THE MOST OFTEN HEARD PHRASES AS TO WHY SOME people don't own a gun is "my wife/husband doesn't want a gun in the house because of the children." This is a common objection toward owning a firearm, and must be addressed in a positive way prior to bringing home a firearm. Unfortunately, I can't convince your "significant other" that you can keep a firearm safely in your house. I can tell you what I have done.

When our son was born, I spent a great deal of time "baby-proofing" our house. I installed cabinet locks to keep him out of the bleach and cleaning stuff under the sink, I installed drawer locks on the kitchen drawers that had knives. I did all this to protect my child from dangerous items in the house. Guns are dangerous too and should always be secured from young hands. There does come a point where you stop locking the knives and reason with your children about things that can hurt them. My son is sixteen years old (at the time of this writing) and the locks on the drawers and cabinets are long gone. Are the poisons and knives any less dangerous? No, he has just been instructed in their proper use, respects that they are lethal, and, more importantly, they don't hold any mystery.

Demystifying your firearms is the best way to prevent a tragedy. A person can be killed with that hammer hanging in your shop. Do you worry about that hammer? Probably not, because it's not "forbidden fruit." Your child doesn't sneak around the house to find a hammer to show his friends. But time and again the airwaves are full of stories where a child has found a gun and shoots someone. Why? Because *you* didn't teach them any better. By not taking away the aspect of "forbidden fruit," your child is much more likely to get into trouble with your firearm. I started showing my son our firearms by age four. I let him know in no uncertain terms that these were dangerous, just like the knives in the kitchen, and he must not ever touch them without father's direct supervision. Furthermore, I explained to him that I'd always take the time to show him or his friends any or all of my guns. All they had to do was ask. To this day, my son shows about as much interest in a new gun in the house as he would a new screwdriver.

As important as "demystifying" your firearm is, it's also incumbent upon you to secure your gun. If you have kids in the house, for goodness' sake don't leave your handgun in the nightstand. They *will* find it. Later in this book we'll look at various strategies for securing your guns in greater detail. All guns in our house are locked in safes. The only exceptions to that are two old WWII bolt-action rifles that hang over the mantel. One of those is nonfunctional, and all the ammunition for the other one is also locked in a safe.

CHAPTER

2

How Does
a Gun Work?

IF YOU'RE GOING TO OWN A FIREARM, IT IS INCUMBENT
on you to know how it works. This section discusses the modern cartridge
and also discusses the "parts" of a gun." We'll build on this knowledge in
later sections.

Bullets, Cartridges, and Shells—Oh My

At the end of the day, a firearm is a device that launches a projectile (made
of lead or lead with a copper jacket) at very high speeds. Now, there are a
myriad of ways that that cartridge can be loaded into a chamber, the powder ignited, and the empty case extracted. The common denominator is the
cartridge itself.

So, what does it take? Well, the first component is the projectile called the "bullet." This is the part that leaves the barrel and strikes whatever the gun was aimed at. See, *the bullet never misses.* It goes exactly where it is pointed (see the "Ten Commandments of Gun Safety").

Having the bullet is not enough. Next you must have the propellant that launches the bullet down the barrel. This propellant is commonly referred to as "gunpowder," which is only half-right. In the beginning, the Chinese created a substance which was refined over the centuries (in a long, long and boring story) to become what we now call "black powder" or "gunpowder." This powder was used in guns right up to 1898 when the first powder made out of a nitrocellulose chemical process was created by Nobel (of the Dynamite/TNT/Nobel Prize—Nobels). The new powder burned much cleaner, so it was called "smokeless powder." That's what's in your everyday cartridge today. If you call it gunpowder, you most likely won't be corrected, but you should know that they aren't exactly the same either.

Next, you need something to make the powder burn. A minister in the early 1800s found that if you struck some forms of fulminate mercury, it would produce a spark hot enough to ignite powder. Thus the percussion cap was born. The percussion cap was a "cup" made of a soft metal (usually tin) that was filled with the "priming compound." Prior to cartridge guns, these "primers" or "caps" were fitted on a firearm's nipple and then a hammer struck the nipple, igniting the powder. The cap splintered and was discarded. Perhaps this is where the phrase "bust a cap" came from to mean fire a gun?

Eventually, Horace Smith and Daniel Baird Wesson figured out that if you took a brass case, installed priming compound, gunpowder (originally black powder, later smokeless), and a bullet, you had a "projectile delivery system" that would be waterproof, could be made cheaply, and thus created the modern cartridge.

The "cartridge case" holds the powder, primer, and bullet together. Until after the Second World War, most were made out of brass. As such, most cartridge cases (by themselves) are usually referred to as "brass" even though they might be made out of steel today.

Today, there are two main variants of cartridges: rimfire and centerfire. The difference between these is largely made up of how the gunpowder is ignited. Individual cartridges are typically referred to as "rounds." Rumor has it that in the Old West, a cowboy who was "down on his luck" could trade a single *round* for a small glass of whiskey. And that is how the "shot glass" got its name and how "buying a round" came into being. However, it's not against a true cowboy's nature to pull your leg either, so take that with a grain of salt.

Rimfire versus CenterFire

The most popular cartridge consumed worldwide is the rimfire .22-Caliber long rifle cartridge. More .22 cartridges are produced than ammunition for all the armies of all the world. The diminutive .22 cartridge is used for hunting small game, killing pests and varmints (up to coyote size), and target practice. Although not recommended due to its poor stopping power, it is also carried as a personal protection round.

In a "rimfire" round the priming compound is poured into the empty case and permitted to dry. The compound settles in the base of the cartridge, around the rim (hence the name). After the compound dries, the cartridge case is filled with powder and caped with a bullet.

When the round is struck sharply on the rim, the priming compound is ignited, thus igniting the powder, and creating a great deal of pressure which pushes the bullet down the barrel. Since the brass cartridge case is permanently dented by the ignition, rimfire cases are unable to be reloaded.

The other major type of cartridge is the centerfire cartridge. In a "centerfire" cartridge, the priming compound is inserted into a recess in the *center* of the cartridge case (see illustration). Since the priming compound (or "primer") is self-contained, spent rounds can be easily removed and the brass reloaded and used again.

Cartridge versus Shell

The fact of the matter is that when you deal with firearms, you'll hear lots of terms . . . many used incorrectly . . . Go figure. For the purpose of this book, a "cartridge" is a self-contained metallic hulled device consisting

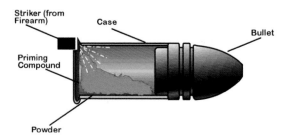

A rimfire cartridge being struck (at the base of the cartridge)

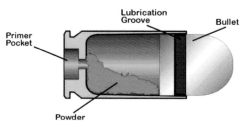

Centerfire cartridge case

of a single projectile, a propellant, and a priming compound. A "shell" is a self-contained cylinder consisting of a priming compound, a propellant, one or more projectiles (separated from the powder by a "wad"). Shells are most commonly used in shotguns; however, some "shot shells" are marketed to be loaded in handguns, primarily for snake and rodent control (these are commonly called "rat shot" or "snake shot"). So when you're talking about a "shotgun," you don't reach for cartridges, you reach for shells.

We'll come back to ammo and cartridges later when we'll look at what kind of ammunition you need to buy for your firearm.

Parts of a Firearm

Back in the time of the U. S. Revolution, there were three parts to every firearm. The barrel, the locking mechanism (or the spring, trigger group, and associated parts to actually fire the gun), and the wooden stock (ever heard the phrase "lock stock, and barrel"?).

Modern firearms are slightly more complicated, but share many of the same components.

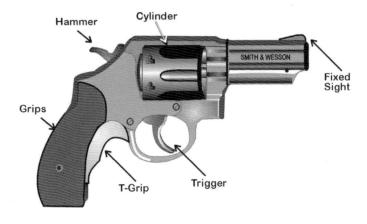

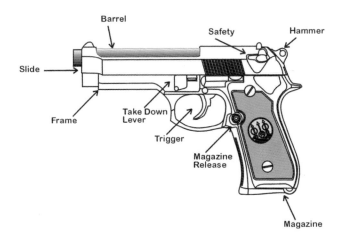

Starting at the back, every firearm must have a mechanism for supporting the weapon. This can be a wooden or synthetic stock for a rifle or shotgun, or a wooden, rubber, stag, or other natural material "grip" for a handgun.

Next there is a place to store the cartridges while they are waiting to be shot. On a revolver, this would be the cylinder. On a rifle or semiautomatic pistol or shotgun, this would be a "magazine." Although some firearms are single-shot affairs and don't have an internal ammunition store.

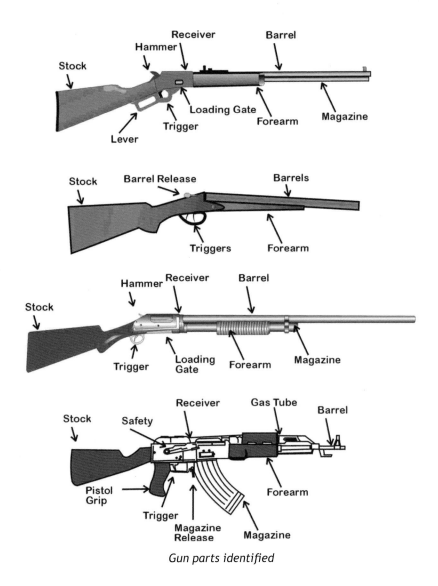

Gun parts identified

Next you have the area on the firearm where the cartridge is contained for detonation. This area is called the "chamber" and must be sufficiently strong to withstand the pressures of the detonation.

Trigger – The trigger's function is to release the "sear" which permits the firing pin to strike the cartridge's primer, thus sending the projectile out of the barrel. The area that protects the trigger from unintentional discharge is called the "trigger guard."

Hammer – The hammer's job is to strike the firing pin (which ignites the primer) or to strike the rim on a rimfire cartridge. The hammer may be manipulated manually (as in an "Old West"–style single-action revolver) or it can be concealed.

Sear – The sear is the mechanical device that transfers the action of the trigger to release the tension on the hammer (or striker) to detonate the primer on the cartridge.

Striker – Certain handguns don't have a hammer. Instead, they have a spring-loaded firing pin called a striker. The Glock family of handguns mainstreamed the use of strikers. Most firearms companies today offer a striker-fired pistol (Smith & Wesson, Glock, Springfield, Kahr, Heckler and Koch, Taurus, etc.).

Barrels – The barrel mates to the firearm's receiver and acts as the staging area for the detonation. After the power has been ignited, grooves (referred to as *rifling*) in the barrel spin the projectile to impart stability as the bullet leaves the barrel. Shotgun barrels are typically "smooth bores," that is, no rifling.

Sights – There are typically two types of sights on firearms today, fixed and adjustable. A fixed sight is very durable and is typically manufactured into the frame. Adjustable sights are typically deployed on competition, target, or hunting handguns to match the aim point of the firearm to the impact for the specific cartridge that is being used.

Cylinder – Cylinders are unique to a certain type of handguns, revolvers. The cylinder holds the cartridges and rotates to line one cartridge up at a time with the barrel.

CHAPTER

3

Types of Guns

NOW THAT WE'VE TAKEN A LOOK AT THE BACKGROUND, we'll explore the three main categories of firearms (handguns, rifles, and shotguns) and break down subdivisions in each category.

Handguns

As the name states, a handgun is designed to be fired by holding the gun with one or both hands, unsupported by the shooter's shoulder. This covers a *broad* range of firearms. From the smallest hide-out gun to truly massive "hand cannons" that fire rifle cartridges. Generally, handguns break down into three categories: revolvers, pistols, and specialty/novelty firearms.

Single action illustrated—top, uncocked, bottom, cocked

Revolvers

The revolver was invented by Samuel Colt in the mid-1800s. A revolver features a "cylinder" that rotates the cartridge into a position where it's ready to be fired. The mechanism for rotating the cylinder is classified by the "action" that results from the user pulling the trigger. As a result, a revolver will always be either a "single action" or a "double action."

SINGLE-ACTION REVOLVERS

The single-action revolver conjures up images of the steely-eyed gun-fighter of the Old West, staring down a rival in the dusty street at high noon. Not that there were really any documented gunfights in the streets of the Old West. Only one such gunfight was ever recorded, but why ruin a good

Iver Johnson top-break revolver

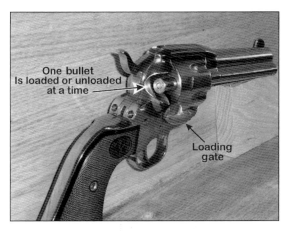

Illustration of single action with open loading gate

legend. The single-action revolver is so named because pulling the trigger only releases the hammer to strike the primer (or the rim of a rimfire) cartridge. Therefore, pulling the trigger only causes a *single action* to occur, hence the name single-action.

This means that in order to fire a single-action revolver, the shooter must first pull back on the hammer until it locks into place. The revolver may then be aimed and fired. In order to fire subsequent times, the shooter must pull the hammer back each time.

Loading a Single Action revolver is usually done by opening a "loading gate" on the side of the revolver or by hinging the entire top of the firearm (as in the case of the Smith & Wesson Schofield revolver). This makes loading the revolver and removing fired (or "spent") cartridges tedious.

Since the single-action revolver is synonymous with the "Old West," some might question why we're discussing it in a book about choosing a firearm to own in the 21st century. The truth is that the single-action never went away. OK, it *almost* went away. The single-action was largely replaced by the double-action revolver. In fact, after World War II, Colt stopped making the single-action revolver. It wasn't until Sturm, Ruger started making their version of the single-action Revolver in the 1950s that the single-action was "reborn." The rise of Cowboy Action Shooting in the 1980s spurred (pardon the pun) growth in single-action revolver collecting, shooting, and competition. Many manufacturers today offer their take on the classic single-action revolver including Colt, Ruger, Taurus, Beretta, Uberti, Charles Daly, and Stoeger. Common barrel lengths for single-action revolvers are four and a half inches, five and a half inches, and seven inches, although some models, referred to as "buntline" models, sported a factory twelve-inch barrel.

So, what does one do with a single-action revolver?

Earlier, we gave a list of possible uses for a firearm. In case you skimmed that chapter, they were (1) personal defense, (2) personal accomplishment/fun/plinking, (3) hunting, and/or (4) collecting. Since the single-action revolver must be cocked before firing each time, it's considered by most to be a poor choice for personal protection. In a stressful situation, it's best not to have to remember to cock your gun. If your firearm purchase is *strictly* for personal defense, you might want to consider the double-action revolver or skip to the "Pistol" section.

Personal accomplishment/fun/plinking—*you bet!* The single-action excels in this role. Cowboy Action Shooting (CAS) and Cowboy Fast Draw competitions use the single-action revolver (CAS actually requires the shooter to have *two* single-action revolvers). Also, a .22-caliber single-action is a great addition for a camping trip (where shooting is permitted) or to eliminate household pests (snakes, rodents, etc.).

Hunting - The single-action design is extremely strong and durable, making it a fine selection for a hunting firearm. The safety of the single-action (remember that it can't go off unless you pull the hammer back) makes it

A Cowboy Action shooter (Bea Itchin' SASS #25123)
shooting her single-action revolver

a good choice for hunting with a handgun. Many manufacturers such as Ruger and Freedom Arms manufacture single-action revolvers specifically for hunting.

Finally collecting. There is a tremendous collector's value to the single-action revolver, but as with any investment, careful study is required before considering any investment.

DOUBLE-ACTION REVOLVERS

The double-action (DA) revolver was developed in the late 1880s as an improvement of the single-action revolver. As the name implies, pulling the trigger on a double-action revolver accomplishes two mechanical actions: (1) it cocks the hammer, and (2) it releases the hammer to strike the primer. The advantage to this mechanism is that the shooter does not have to alter

A collection of single-action firearms

Open double-action revolver

their grip on the firearm to cock and fire the weapon (as was required on most single-actions). Early double-action revolvers suffered from delicate mechanisms which were prone to breakage. Thus the SA saw service long into the new century (that's the 1900s).

The first successful DA revolvers were offered from Smith & Wesson (S&W). The chief advantage of Smith revolvers were the swing out cylinder which made loading and unloading the handgun much more efficient.

Modern DA revolvers are suitable for all shooting purposes. Many personal defense experts consider the double-action revolver the best choice for personal defense, especially for the novice shooter. This is chiefly because the DA revolver is simple to operate. Once the revolver is loaded, the shooter just has to aim and pull the trigger. It's the original "point and click" user interface! Pistols (that is, those handguns that are fed by an internal magazine) rely on recoil to load the next round into the chamber. This means that unless the shooter is accomplished with the firearm, they could easily induce a failure to feed the next cartridge. When this happens, the gun becomes useless for defense until the jam is cleared. Conversely, in the double-action revolver, the next round is rotated into position as a result of the trigger being pulled. Should a double-action revolver misfire, you have but to pull the trigger again.

Choosing a revolver for personal defense comes back to the idea of matching the firearm to the defense situation. For example, if the user intends to carry the handgun daily, and typically wears blue jeans and T-shirts, a small lightweight revolver would be a better choice than a large-frame revolver with a four-inch barrel. On the other hand, if the main application for the revolver is to reside in a nightstand or safe in the bedroom, then a four-inch barrel offers a longer "sight radius,[2]" which makes it much easier to shoot accurately.

Long, Heavy Pull versus Short, Light Pull

On a double-action revolver, the shooter may fire the revolver in one of two ways: traditional double-action or single-action (unless the revolver is a double action only). Traditional double action starts with the hammer fully down against the frame. As the shooter pulls the trigger, force is exerted against the hammer spring until the sear trips and the hammer springs forward to strike the primer. Since the hammer has to "pull" the hammer through the entire stroke, it typically takes about twelve pounds of force to perform this action, and the trigger must travel through the entire pull. Conversely, for a single-action pull, the shooter first pulls the hammer back (just like on the single-action revolver you've already read about). Pulling back the hammer until it locks accomplishes the first part of the DA trigger pull so that a much smaller amount of force is required to finish pulling the trigger the rest of the distance. Typically, this is two to five pounds. Note that as the hammer is pulled back, the trigger also travels part of the way back. So, a single-action pull not only requires less force but is also a shorter pull.

---

2 Sight radius – The firearm's sight radius is the distance measured from the front sight to the rear sight. On a short barrel, a small percentage change has a greater effect on the impact of a bullet than a longer sight radius.

Smith & Wesson Model 60—J-frame

When to use which? It's really up to the shooter. Most accomplished revolver shooters will tend to shoot double-action because they don't have to shift their grip on the gun in order to complete the firing sequence. Many newer or target shooters prefer the light, crisp, single-action mode.

Frame Sizes

Most manufacturers of revolvers build their products on a standardized frame. The frame is the metal that holds the action and supports the cylinder and the barrel. By having a standard frame, only the cylinder, barrel, and a few small internal parts need to be changed to produce the firearm in a different caliber.[3] Smith & Wesson pioneered this concept. In their parlance, they have assigned letter designations to the frame sizes. In fact, many other manufacturers have copied the concept and have even adopted S&W's designations. The smallest revolver that S&W currently offers is the J-frame. J-frame revolvers are typically small-caliber revolvers (smaller than .357) and typically hold five

---

3 Caliber refers to the diameter of the bore of the firearm. This number can be represented in metric (e.g., 9 mm) or hundredths of an inch (such as .357).

shots. Barrel lengths are usually limited to two to three inches since most small-frame revolvers are intended for concealed carry. Example of "small-frame" revolvers are the Smith & Wesson Model 60, Model 36, Model 640, Taurus Model 85, Ruger SP 101, and the Colt Cobra Special.

Frames may be made of steel, aluminum, titanium, or other exotic metals (S&W is fond of scandium). Steel frames are heavier and absorb the shock of firing (recoil) better than lighter materials. Lighter guns are easier to carry. Remember, if a gun is too heavy, it tends to be left behind, and a gun in the "glove compartment" is no use to you if you really need it where you are.

Smith & Wesson Small-Frame Revolver Models and Weights		
Model	Frame Material	Weight (unloaded)
340PD	scandium	12 oz.
642	aluminum	15 oz.
60	steel	22 oz.

The next size frame are the "medium frame" revolvers. In S&W designations, these would be the K- and L-frame revolvers. K/L-frame revolvers are the workhorse of most revolver lines. Up until the 1980s, most police officers in the United States carried a medium-frame revolver (typically made by S&W, Colt, or Ruger) with a four-inch barrel. While a four-inch barrel is still an excellent choice, other common lengths vary from two to eight inches. Two- to three-inch barrels are an excellent choice for concealed carry/personal protection. Barrel lengths up to four inches work well if concealment is not an issue (such as in a nightstand, or carried in a car's glove compartment[4]). Barrels over four inches are best suited for hunting and target shooting/competition.

Hundreds of thousands of K/L-frame revolvers have been made since the 1930s. Most are still in use today. In 2005, S&W discontinued the K-frame in favor of the reinforced L-frame. The L-frame was designed especially to handle the higher pressures of the .357 cartridge. One note,

---

4 Where legal

Smith & Wesson—Model 66, F-frame (medium frame)

there are thousands of K-frame" .357 revolvers. Most were shot with .38 ammo, but carried with .357 for duty. These guns are fine; however, a steady diet of strong .357 loads will hasten wear on the revolver. The L-frame is made to shoot *primarily* .357 loads. Examples of medium-frame revolvers include S&W Military and Police (or M&P) revolver, Model 10, Model 13, Model 64, 65, 66, 686, 619, 620 (and many more). Medium-frame revolvers from other manufacturers include Ruger GP 100, Colt Trooper, Colt Diamondback, and the Taurus Model 65, and Model 66.

The next larger DA revolver frame is the "N-frame." The N-frame is considered a combat-sized revolver. The large size of the frame permits calibers up to 45 to be carried. The most famous N-frame is the Model 29 Smith & Wesson. This revolver, chambered in .44 Magnum, was carried by Clint Eastwood in the *Dirty Harry* movies.

The size and weight of the N-frame revolvers make them less than ideal for concealed carry, but excellent for competition, hunting, and collecting. Examples of large-frame revolvers include the S&W Models 29, 629, 25, 625, Ruger Redhawk, Colt Anaconda, and the Raging Bull line from Taurus.

Smith & Wesson Model 65 Ladysmith – K frame revolver

Smith & Wesson Model 625—large-frame revolver in .45 Colt

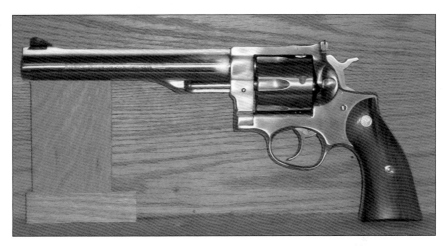

*Ruger Redhawk in .44 Magnum caliber—large-frame, double-action revolver—
from the collection of Claud Summers*

Finally there are the "super large frame" revolvers. In 2005 S&W introduced the latest "most powerful handgun in the world," the S&W .500
which was built on its "X-frame." This .50-caliber handgun is intended for
hunting dangerous game (bears, lion, etc.) in rugged environments where a
rifle might be unruly (such as dense forest or swamps).

DOUBLE-ACTION-ONLY REVOLVERS

The final, major type of revolver is the double-action-only revolver. This
revolver type is a modification of the traditional double-action revolver.
On most double-action revolvers, the shooter may elect to thumb back the
hammer manually (instead of just pulling the trigger). When the shooter
does this, the gun becomes, in effect, a *single-action revolver*.

Some revolvers have their hammer cut down or housed internally. This
is typically done so the gun does not "snag" on clothing when it is drawn
from a pocket or holster. This type of action is referred to as "double action
only," because the shooter does not have the option of pulling back on the
hammer.

Smith & Wesson Model 640, double-action-only revolver

The Utility of the .357

Most everyone has heard of the .357 Magnum cartridge. What most people don't know is that the .357 Magnum is a fairly new cartridge (being invented in the 1930s, hey! new is relative). The cartridge was invented as a response to the then-anemic performance of the .38 special bullet when loaded with a lead bullet.

Pushing a 125-grain[5] bullet at over 1,200 feet per second, the .357 is a potent round for both personal protection and even hunting up to deer-size game.

The .357 Magnum was developed by lengthening the .38 Special case. As a result, any revolver that is chambered for .357 will also fire .38 Special (or even .38 S&W) ammunition. This makes the .357 revolver even more utilitarian. Light (and inexpensive) .38 Special loads can be used for practice

---

5   Grain is a unit of weight used to weigh out both projectiles and propellant. One grain equals 0.002285 ounce, or .065 gram.

and "plinking." Heavier loads can be used for competition and self-defense. Other specialty loads, such as shot shells, can be used for snake and rodent control.

All these factors combine to make the .357 revolver one of the best choices for any firearms owner.

Pistols

A "pistol" is a type of handgun that loads rounds into the barrel through a removable or fixed "magazine." Typically this magazine is loaded through the bottom of the grip. *"You mean an automatic?"* The author cringes. One of the most common mispronouncements in all of the shooting sports is referring to a "self-loading pistol" as an "automatic." *Technically,* the term "automatic" means that when you pull the trigger, the firearm fires repeatedly until empty or the trigger is released. Or a "fully automatic machine gun" if you prefer. The ordinary citizen in the United States cannot purchase a

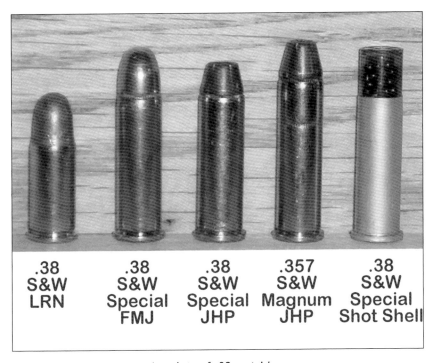

.38	.38	.38	.357	.38
S&W	S&W	S&W	S&W	S&W
LRN	Special	Special	Magnum	Special
	FMJ	JHP	JHP	Shot Shell

A variety of .38 cartridges

"fully automatic" weapon without purchasing a special license. The purchase of this license includes an extensive background check to make sure that the buyer is not a "bad guy." *So why does everyone call it an automatic?* Face it, people will shorten anything . . . as anybody named "Robert" knows.

What they *mean* to say is "semiautomatic." The definition of "semi-automatic" is that every time the shooter pulls the trigger, the firearm fires once, then reloads itself and resets the trigger. Releasing the trigger and pulling it again repeats the cycle until the magazine is empty.

So, a pistol uses a clip, right? Another *slight* cringe. Technically it's a magazine. A "clip" is a piece of spring steel that holds rounds together and is placed into a firearm. A "magazine" is a spring-loaded container that pushes rounds into the chamber one at a time. Referring to a "magazine" as a "clip" isn't correct, but everyone does it . . . *even me.*

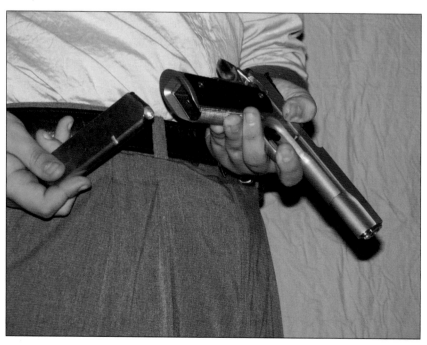

A magazine being inserted into a single-action semiautomatic pistol

Automatics were created as an answer to the slow, awkward loading of the single-action revolver. By carrying magazines, the shooter could reload their weapon in record time.

HOW DOES IT WORK?

Most semiautomatic pistols work by using the energy created by the detonation of the round to move a "slide" to the rear of the unit. The rearward movement of the slide ejects the (now spent) shell that is in the chamber.[6] A spring mounted in the slide compresses as the slide moves to the rear. Eventually, the spring becomes fully compressed and starts to move the slide back (forward). As the slide travels forward, it picks up a round from the magazine and feeds it back into the chamber.

So consider this. The recoil of the round being fired is critical to the operation of a semiautomatic pistol. This means that the operator must hold the pistol very firmly for it to operate correctly. Permitting the pistol to move in the shooter's hand can result in lost energy. This can cause a myriad of problems. These problems include not extracting the empty cartridge in the chamber, or not feeding the fresh round from the magazine, or misfeeding the round into the chamber (or "stove piping").

The concern is that should a round not feed correctly into the chamber of the pistol, the operator had to clear the jam before they could continue to fire. This isn't a big deal . . . *as long as no one is firing at you.*

TYPES OF SEMIAUTOMATIC PISTOLS

As mentioned in the previous section different types of revolvers are defined by their operation (single action/double action/double action only). Pistols too are classified by their action.

Just like revolvers, there are single action, double action, double action only pistols. There is also a class of pistols called "striker fired." Each type of pistol will be covered in its own section in this chapter.

---

6 By a slide-mounted "hook shaped" spring called an extractor

Ruger Mark II .22-caliber single-action semiautomatic pistol—from the collection of Claud Summers

SINGLE-ACTION SEMIAUTOMATIC PISTOLS

The single-action semiautomatic pistol is one of the most revered hand-guns in the shooting world. Many "old-timers" (and lots of "young bucks" and "camo commandos") will tell you that the single-action auto (really "semiauto," right?) is by far the single best invention up to and including toilet paper and sliced bread. I wouldn't call them wrong. I wouldn't call them right either. See, it all goes back to the same question, "What do you want to *do* with your gun?"

The single-action semiautomatic shares a key characteristic with the single-action revolver. That being, the "hammer" must be pulled back every time the pistol is fired. Now, I know that you're thinking, *I've never seen "the Duke," or Humphrey Bogart, or even Don Johnson, Steven Segal, or Arnold pulling back the hammer on their pistol after each shot.* And you'd be right.

The photo above shows what happens after a semiautomatic pistol is fired. The recoil of the escaping gas (as it pushes the bullet out of the barrel) forces the "slide" backward on the pistol's "frame." As the slide goes back, it pushes the hammer down, and out of the way, thus cocking the hammer in the process. Eventually, a spring that is mounted in the slide pulls the slide

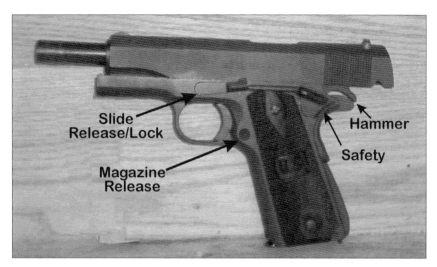

1911 with slide locked open

forward again, but the hammer stays cocked, and ready for a very light, crisp pull of the trigger to release it to start the process over.

Therefore, on a single action, semiautomatic pistol, if the hammer is at rest against the frame (down), as in the picture below, pulling the trigger does nothing. The gun cannot fire unless the hammer is manually pulled back or is reset by the slide being pulled back.

From a personal protection standpoint, this means that any single-action pistol must be carried with the hammer back on a live cartridge (because you wouldn't want to have to thumb back the hammer prior to use). Remember, just like a single-action revolver, or double-action revolver, when the hammer is locked back, it only takes a small amount of force for it to trip the "sear" and fire. This is why *almost* all single-action semiautomatic pistols have a manual safety (see picture below).

The manual safety prevents an "accidental discharge" of the weapon while in the holster or before the shooter is ready to fire. The important thing to remember when carrying and shooting a single-action semiautomatic is to get the muzzle of the gun pointed safely downrange before disengaging the safety. Now is the time for some more jargon. When the hammer is pulled back and the safety is engaged (on a single-action pis-

Detonics USA Model 9-11-01 single-action semiautomatic pistol n .45 ACP

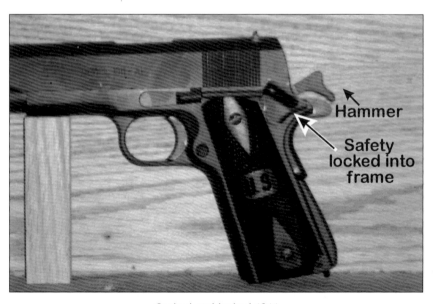

Hammer

Safety
locked into
frame

Cocked and locked 1911

tol), the gun is said to be "cocked and locked." That is, the hammer is back (cocked) and the safety is engaged (locked). This is how the 1911 pistol was carried by our combat troops for over seventy years (and is still carried by many special forces troops and police SWAT teams).

Why choose a single-action semiautomatic pistol?

OK, I'll say it! As a firearms enthusiast and instructor, I seldom recommend a single-action semiautomatic pistol as a shooter's "first" firearm. This is especially true if the shooter wants the gun primarily for personal protection. There are two reasons for this. The first is that single-action automatics are extremely sensitive to malfunctions if the shooter doesn't apply a firm grip (which is unlikely for an inexperienced shooter) and secondly because they must be carried "cocked and locked" to be truly effective in a self-defense solution.

Single-action semiautomatics really shine as target and competition firearms, as well as personal protection and police/military applications. The light crisp trigger makes this type of pistol *very* accurate in the hands of the experienced user.

This doesn't mean that I don't advocate owning, shooting, or even carrying a single-action pistol. If proper care is taken and the shooter is intimately familiar with the SA pistol, then that's what they should carry. But just because "the Duke" used one in *Sands of Iwo Jima* is not the best reason to buy one. Not that that's a *bad* reason.

DOUBLE-ACTION/SINGLE-ACTION AND DAO SEMIAUTOMATIC PISTOLS

Like the double-action revolvers, pistols can also come in double-action variants. Also like a DA revolver, pulling the trigger accomplishes two tasks. The first being to draw back the hammer (in preparation to strike the priming compound), and to release the hammer. It is after the trigger releases the hammer that things get interesting for the double-action semiautomatic.

Just like a single-action pistol, when the trigger is fired, the inertia from the fired round moves the slide rearward on "rails" built into the slide. This ejects the spent case in the chamber, cocks the hammer, and then (as the slide moves forward) picks up a fresh cartridge from the magazine. It's what happens to the hammer when the slide is fully forward with a round in the chamber, or "in battery" that differentiates the types of DA pistols.

There are three main types of double-action pistols: traditional double action/single-action, double-action-only, and striker fired. Naturally, there is an endless array of minor variations; however, this should suffice for a "introductory book."

TRADITIONAL DA/SA

History and Trivia

In the late 1920s and into the 1930s extensive research was undertaken to make the semiautomatic pistol safer to carry. One of the companies that was first successful was the Carl Walther company with their "Police Pistol" (or *Polizei Pistole*), which was first released in 1931. The success of this pistol lead to the creation of a smaller pistol for detectives and undercover police. This pistol was designated the *Polizei Pistole Kriminal* or PPK. This is still

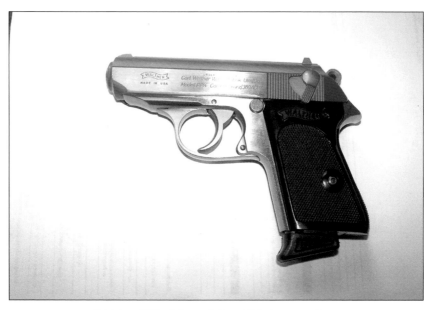

Walther PPK with traditional DA decock safety,
from the collection of Don S. Smith

one of the best known pistols in use today, largely due to the fact that James Bond used this pistol in many of the Bond movies.

How does a double-action semiautomatic work?

The double-action semiautomatic pistol is significantly different in operation from the double-action revolver. Early marketing by gun manufacturers referred to the action as "double action"; however, a much more accurate description would be "double action/single-action." Here's why . . . In a double-action revolver, each pull of the trigger results in the hammer being pulled completely through its cycle, and returning to the exact same point where it began.

But! In a DA/SA pistol, the first shot cocks and fires the weapon. As the slide comes back, it recocks the hammer (just like a single-action semiautomatic pistol). The hammer stays back, and is "recocked" on every subsequent shot. So while the first round is fired "double action," every other round in the magazine is fired "single-action." This then becomes abbreviated as "double-action/single-action."

The Hammer Drop Safety and Decocker Only

So it just couldn't be that simple. As we reviewed earlier, the safety mechanism on a single-action pistol (like the 1911) locks the action and keeps the gun from firing. The firearm is typically then carried with the hammer back on a *live* cartridge with only the safety to stop it. This was seen as a potential safety problem. This is one of the main reasons that police organizations resisted the semiautomatic pistol for so long.

On *most* double-action pistols, engaging the safety safely lowers the hammer (without making contact with the firing pin). The pistol is then "on safe" *until the shooter moves the mechanism to its "fire" position* (see picture of Walther PPK at the beginning of this chapter). From here, the first shot will be the long double-action pull. Pistols that feature this type of safety include the Walther pistols (P38 and PPK), the Smith & Wesson second- and third-generation semiautomatic pistols, the Ruger "P-series" pistols, and too many others to mention. The important thing to remember about this type of DA pistols is that the safety must be moved before the pistol will fire. This brings us to the "decock only" type of safety.

Walther P38 from the collection of Don S. Smith

Decock Only

Decock-only (or decocker) semiautomatic pistols shoot in the same manner as DA/SA pistols. The first shot is a long DA pull that cocks and releases the hammer while subsequent shots are light single-action. In fact, most decock safeties look identical to a "regular" DA/SA safety. The difference is that once the decock lever is manipulated, it safely drops the hammer, and then returns to its regular "off-safe" setting. So the "safety" on a decock-only semiauto does not keep the firearm from firing. It just drops the hammer *safely*.

Many law enforcement agencies find a decocker DA pistol to be the best choice for their officers (or a striker-fired pistol like a Glock). The officer can simply point their sidearm at the target and pull the trigger. When they have finished firing, they decock the weapon and reholster. The pistol is now hammered down on a cartridge, but cannot ignite the cartridge without a long, deliberate pull of the trigger. Decock semiautomatic pistols make an excellent choice for personal protection.

SIG Sauer and Ruger are two gun companies who have enthusiastically embraced the "decock only" concept although Smith & Wesson, Heckler and Koch (H&K), Beretta, Ceska Zbrojovka (CZ), and too many others to list.

DOUBLE-ACTION ONLY SEMIAUTOMATIC PISTOLS

This leads us to the type of semiautomatic pistols that are most like double-action revolvers, the double-action-only (DAO) pistols. The DAO pistol was developed in response to a long string of embarrassing law enforcement officer (LEO) shootings when the semiautomatic pistol started to overtake the double-action revolver in the 1980s and 1990s. At the time, LEOs were familiar with their DA revolvers. Heck they'd had them for almost one hundred years! There were many accidental discharges with the "newfangled" semiautomatic actions (be they cocked and locked, DA/SA, or even decock only). Another reported problem was officers getting shot because they forgot to deactivate the safety on their guns. The idea then became to manufacture a "hybrid" firearm that would combine the simple operation of a double-action-only revolver with the high magazine capacity of a semiautomatic pistol. Thus was born the DAO semiautomatic pistol. One of the first agencies to request this firearm was the New York City police force. At that time, the force required over five thousand guns. This was a very attractive enticement for gun manufacturers to offer guns to fit their needs.

Operationally, the DAO functions similarly to the double-action semiautomatic. A magazine is inserted into the base of the grip. The slide is pulled to the rear and allowed to move forward under spring tension. The slide moving forward strips a cartridge from the magazine and loads it into the chamber. The principal difference is that the hammer does not stay cocked. As the slide moves forward, the hammer follows the slide to its "rest" position against the slide. This would be the equivalent of operating the slide on a traditional double-action semiauto and then manipulating the decock safety.

So DAO are for law enforcement only? No. Many shooters find the predictability of the exact same trigger pull, for every shot in the magazine, to be easier to learn than the traditional "long pull/short pull" of a traditional DA/SA. Additionally, the DAO semiautomatic makes an excellent self-defense weapon as there are no external safeties to manipulate when the shooter is most distracted (that is, being attacked).

SIG Sauer 229 DAK in .40 S&W caliber

STRIKER FIRED—"SAFE ACTION"™ SEMIAUTOMATIC PISTOLS

The final main type of semiautomatic pistol is the striker-fired pistol. While this action type has been around for years, it was really popularized by a Austrian plastics manufacturer named Gaston Glock. Legend has it that Mr. Glock overheard some Austrian army officers grousing about the poor sidearms they were issued. Glock set about to "build a better mouse trap" *and succeeded!* Up until this time, most semiautomatic pistols had around sixty-plus parts. Gaston Glock designed a handgun that had just thirty-three! Additionally, the frame of the handgun and several internal parts were made of a high-strength polymer (not really plastic), thus reducing weight and manufacturing costs.

Rather than relying on a falling hammer to drive a firing pin into the primer, a striker-fired handgun draws back the firing pin (under spring tension) and releases it to drive forward to strike the primer. This reduces the total number of parts required and the total number of moving parts.

One of the keys to the success of the Striker-fired pistol is the smooth trigger pull. The feel of the trigger is very consistent through the whole stroke. Here's how it works for most "striker fired" pistols. The user pulls back on the trigger which activates the sear mechanism. The sear mechanism pulls back on a spring that supports the striker (firing pin). When the sear gets to the release point, it springs forward, detonating the cartridge primer and firing the shot. The slide behaves like most other semiautomatic pistols in that it extracts the spent cartridge brass, partially resets the trigger, and then loads another round into the chamber. The shooter then is free to repeat the process.

Safe Action™?

The term **"Safe Action™"** is a trademark and trade name for Glock's triumvirate of safety features. Simply put, you can't set off the Glock's striker mechanism unless you (1) depress the *"safety lever"* on the trigger, (2) the long pull of the trigger then overcomes the *"firing pin safety,"* and the (3) moves past the *"drop safety"*.[7] Only until all these tasks have been accomplished will the Glock fire.

But Glock isn't the only game in town. In the twenty years since its introduction, Glock has risen from complete obscurity to over a 60 percent market share of U.S. law enforcement holsters! The rest of the gun industry hasn't been sitting idly by. Smith & Wesson makes two striker-based firearms, the *sigma* (which follows the Glock very closely in operation, form, and function) and the new Military and Police (or M&P) model. Taurus has the PT 24/7 series of striker-fired pistols. Springfield Armory has the

---

7 A "drop safety" is a mechanism that prevents the striker from contacting the primer if the firearm is accidentally dropped.

Glock 17—"Safe Action" 9 mm semiautomatic

excellent Croatian imported XD Series handguns. SIG, CZ, and H&K also offer excellent striker-fired handguns.

One of the main benefits of a striker-fired and polymer-frame gun is its weight. A fully loaded Glock Model 17 with a five-inch barrel and seventeen rounds of 9 mm ammunition weighs thirty-two ounces. A Smith & Wesson 686 double-action revolver that only holds six rounds weighs forty ounces, *empty*.

So striker-fired handguns are the best?

Well, it still goes back to the same question . . . "What do you want to use your handgun for?" While a striker-fired gun is terrific, many just don't like the feel of their action. Striker-fired guns are terrific for self-defense, competition, most are marginal for hunting, which leaves collecting, and frankly, you've seen one black polymer-framed gun, you've pretty much seen them all. Still, if you carry a gun all day, every day, many come to appreciate the savings in weight.

Specialty/Novelty

Yes, there is an "other" section in this book for the handguns that don't fit neatly into the other categories.

HUNTING

First would be the "hand cannons." Single-shot, bolt-action or break-open handguns such as the Remington XP series, or the Thompson Center Contenders. These guns are highly specialized and are intended for the serious hunter and competitor. The Thompson Center offering, the Contender, features easily changeable barrels that make the guns very versatile. By just changing out the barrels, the shooter can go from .22 rimfire through .45-70. Put another way, one handgun can go from plinking at tin cans to a weapon that is suitable to hunt bear and moose.

A collection of Thompson Center hunting pistols

DERRINGERS

Almost as easily identifiable as the single-action revolver is the over/under derringer. The derringer was actually invented by a man named "Henry Deringer" but gained an extra *R* when Remington started producing the firearms at the turn of the century. While the most popular patter is the tip-up, break-open design, the name "derringer" has come to include a small inexpensive firearm usually in a smaller caliber.

Cowboy Action Shooting resurrected interest in the derringer. Companies such as Bond Arms and American Derringer Company have led the way in manufacturing well-made derringers that will last a lifetime. But a caution. Derringers are a weapon of "last resort." Made to be fired at a distance of feet rather than yards. As a result, they are typically not too long on accuracy and brutal from a recoil standpoint. In short, while small, they should not be considered for self-defense.

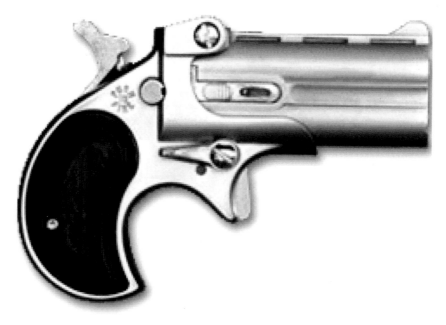

Cobra derringer

CUSTOM COMPETITION HANDGUNS

Several manufacturers make custom guns that are used solely for Olympic or other competition. Companies like Hammerli and SIG, Beretta, Steyr-Mannlicher, and Walter all make hand-fitted firearms for the competitive market.

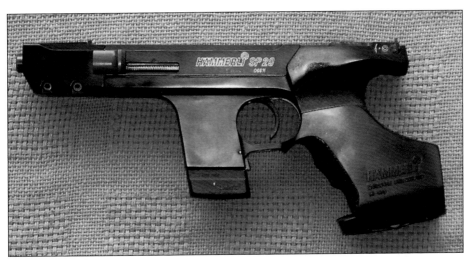

Hammerli SP 20 target pistol as advertised on the Internet

Rifles and Carbines

Moving up from handguns are "long guns." Long guns include both rifles and shotguns and are defined as any weapon that is designed to be fired by bracing the weapon against the shoulder. In this section we'll examine the common types of rifles and carbines, styles and uses. The next chapter will focus on shotguns. Remember that this is a "beginner's guide," and not the "end all be all" on every long gun made. If you want that, go to your nearest "big box" bookstore and cruise the "coffee table" books. You'll find more than you can shake a stick at.

There are as many, if not more, producers of rifles and carbines as there are of handguns. Rifles can trace their lineage back over five hundred years to the first brass and iron tube "hand cannons" that were produced in Europe. In fact, the oldest continuously operated company of all industries is an arms maker. Beretta has been in continuous operation over five hundred years and has been making firearms since 1526.

Most early long gun development was driven by the military. Back in the day, many countries ran state-controlled industries called "arsenals" where arms were produced instead of buying firearms produced by public or private companies. Even the United States had its own arsenals. Two of the most famous were located in Springfield, Massachusetts, and Harpers Ferry, Virginia (of the famed song about abolitionist John Brown).

So what makes a rifle? All rifles have certain aspects in common. They all have at least one barrel, some have two. Said barrel has spiral grooves cut into the inside. These grooves are called "rifling" (hence the name rifle). The purpose of the grooves is to impart spin to the projectile (bullet) as it is forced from the barrel. This makes the projectile fly more accurately and further. Long guns with cut rifling have been around since the mid-1860s and first saw widespread action in the American Civil War. Prior to that time, long guns were just smooth tubes of steel. The correct term for these types of long guns were "muskets."

Early rifles were big. In fact the standard British musket (later rifle), the "Brown Bess" was sixty-two inches long and weighed almost nine pounds (more with a bayonet). It was realized early that not all troops in combat needed or could wield such a large weapon. The horse-mounted cavalry was the first to recognize that they needed a shorter weapon, a carbine, that would shoot, load, and just plain carry better on a horse. Also, the fella bringing up the food to the troops who *may* come in contact with the enemy needed a gun, but didn't need to struggle with one almost as long as he was tall! So the term "carbine" has come to be defined as a rifle that has been shortened for use by specialized troops. Even today our military in Iraq makes use of rifles (M16) and carbines (M4, which looks like a shortened M16). Armored troops, noncommissioned officers, officers, cooks, communications, logistics, combat engineers are all examples of troops who may make use of carbines over rifles.

On the "nonmilitary" side, the first repeating rifles were the lever actions that were designed by Winchester and Marlin in the United States. As the rifle developed, new actions, such as the "bolt action" and "pump action," were developed. World wars intervened to drive the invention of semiautomatic rifles and assault rifles.

Each one of these types of firearms will be examined in this chapter.

Lever-Action Rifles

A lever-action rifle utilizes a fixed tubular magazine that is slung under the barrel (to hold the rounds) and a lever mechanism to load the rounds into the chamber. As the shooter moves the lever down, a "lifter" opens the magazine, permitting a single cartridge to enter. Also, as the lever is lowered, the rifle's bolt is drawn to the rear and cocks the hammer. If a round is in the chamber, the "extractor" pulls the round or spent brass from the chamber and throws it clear of the firearm. Pulling the lever back to the closed position raises the lifter (with the cartridge from the magazine) so that the bolt will push it into the chamber as the lever completes its cycle. At this point the rifle is ready to be fired.

One drawback of the lever-action rifle is that by having a tubular magazine, only flat-nose shells can be used in the magazine. This is because the base (primer) of the first round rests against the nose of the second round. Therefore, if significant recoil is encountered or the rifle is dropped (and pointy rounds were used), all the rounds in the magazine could detonate at one time. Having to fire "flat nosed" rounds in the lever-action rifle has always limited its effectiveness in hunting game at long distances. In fact, most people who hunt with a lever-action rifle try to stay within two hundred yards.

The first successful lever-action rifle was developed by Tyler Henry in 1860. The rifle was unusual by today's standards because of its ammunition. It fired a .44-caliber *rimfire* cartridge. This rifle did see some use in the Civil War. Southern troops referred to it as "that damned Yankee rifle that you load on Sunday and shoot all week."

Modern reproduction of the "Henry" rifle

The Henry rifle was very successful, but did have some drawbacks. Chief amongst them was the fact that the shooter had to hold the metal magazine tube which had a tendency to get rather hot after extended fire.

After Oliver Winchester purchased the rights to produce the Henry, he had an "improved Henry" rifle developed and released in 1866. The "1866 Winchester" was the first lever-action that most people would recognize as having all the traits of a "modern" lever-action rifle. It added the wood "fore stock" and a loading gate to load cartridges into the magazine. Due to the shiny brass frame of the Winchester 1866, the plains Indians often referred to this rifle as "the yellow boy." The name endures to this day.

Photo of Winchester 1866—EMF reproduction

Winchester 1873, 1892, and 1894—and Beyond

Time moved on and the Winchester line improved. The 1873 Winchester was the first Winchester lever gun that chambered a centerfire cartridge. Known as "the gun that won the West," the 1873 was one of the most popular guns on the frontier. It's also one of the only guns ever to have a movie made about it! Winchester '73 was made in 1950 and starred Jimmy Stewart and a very young *and slim* Shelley Winters.

The 1892 did away with the toggle action and went to the more modern lifter. Finally the 1894 was considered the penultimate lever-action rifle. The 1894 was the first Winchester rifle to be chambered for the "then new" .30-30 round, which combined a .30-caliber round with thirty grains of black powder. A tribute to the success of the 1894 is that is was made continuously from 1894 to 2006, and may be made again in the future.

Photo of Winchester 1866—EMF reproduction

Winchester made other lever-action rifles over the years. Calibers from .22 rimfire to the thumping .405 Winchester were loaded. Sadly, as of spring 2006 the Winchester plant in Hartford, Connecticut, closed its doors. Many of the early-model Winchester lever-actions can still be purchased from Italian and Brazilian manufacturers and their U.S. importers. Look for brands such as Legacy Sports International (LSI), Uberti, Taylor and Company, European American Arms (EAA), and Navy Arms.

Marlin Lever-actions

Another dominate lever-action manufacturer was Marlin Firearms of Hartford Connecticut. John Marlin was an employee of Winchester who went out on his own in the 1880s. Since then, Marlin has produced more .22 rimfire rifles than any other U.S. manufacturer. This was not at the expense of larger caliber rifle cartridges. From .22 to .480 Marlin, the hits just keep coming.

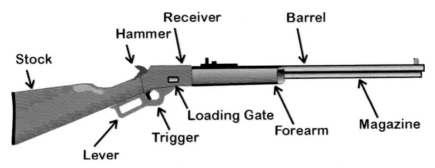

Drawing of Marlin 1894 Cowboy II lever-action rifle

Why Are Lever Guns Still Used?

The lever gun is still popular with all facets of the shooting public. Hunters like the robust yet simple action that permits rapid follow-up shots in a light gun. Shooters love the balance and light handling of the lever-action. Competitors in Cowboy Action Shooting can work the lever-action rifle with blazing speeds. It is not uncommon for a "cowboy" to be able to fire ten rounds in just over four seconds! The rich history of the lever-action makes them fun to collect (depending on how deep your wallet is). Finally, the simple pleasure of "plinking" with a box of .22s and a rimfire lever-action rifle is a joy in itself.

The author (Rolan Kraps, SASS #24084 Life) firing his Marlin 1894 "Cowboy II" model
Lever-action rifle at a Cowboy Action Shooting Match in 2005

Other Lever-actions

So Winchester, Marlin, and a handful of replica manufacturers (more commonly referred to as "clones") aren't the only ones making lever-action rifles today. Browning Arms, Ruger, and the New Henry Rifle company all make fine lever-action rifles.

Bolt-Action Rifles

Bolt-action rifles were the mainstay of most of the world's armies from the turn of the century (that's the 20th century) until World War II. The bolt action dates back to the beginning of the cartridge era. After the Civil War, the metallic cartridge really took off in popularity, and every army needed to throw away their "cap and ball" weapons and gain the superior firepower of the modern cartridge.

One of the most successful designers was Peter Paul Mauser. Herr Mauser's invention was the "bolt action." The steel bolt contains the firing mechanism, locks to keep it from flying out of the gun when the gun is fired, and an extractor for the removal of spent shells from the breech.

Eventually, Mauser and other designers hit on the idea that one could store a magazine under the action. The spring-fed magazine pushed up a new shell every time an old shell was ejected. This is the most common type of bolt action available today.

A chief advantage of the bolt action is its strength. Locking "lugs" on the face of the bolt mate with the chamber, making a very solid platform from which to fire. This makes bolt-action rifles very accurate. This is why many hunters, professional target shooters, and snipers choose bolt actions over other actions (such as semiautomatic). Consider this. The U.S. Military could have any weapon made for an ultraaccurate sniper rifle and they choose a bolt-action rifle.

This doesn't mean that you have to be "the great white hunter" to own a bolt-action rifle. Bolt actions are a terrific way to introduce new shooters to the sport. This is due to the fact that having an open bolt is a clear indication that the rifle is *"clear"* and ready for loading or storage. Companies such as Marlin, Savage, Winchester, Ruger, CZ, and Rogue Rifle Company's Chipmunk are excellent starter bolt action .22s.

Due to the accuracy advantage that is offered by Bolt-action rifles, many shooters and hunters will opt to fit them with a scope. In fact, so many that

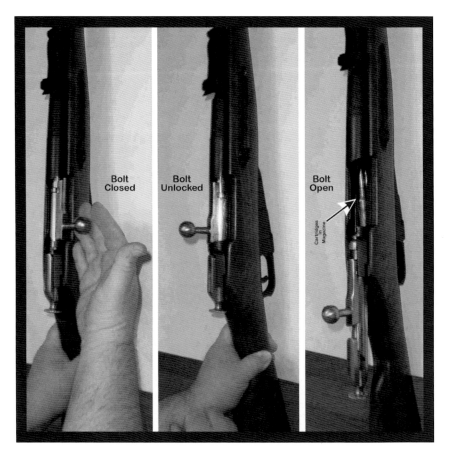

Mosin-Nagant 91/30 rifle showing bolt operation

for most bolt-action rifles front and rear sights (often referred to as "iron sights") are an option.

Short Action versus Long Action

The terms "long action" and "short action" describe the type of cartridges that the bolt-action rifle is designed to shoot. Many cartridges serve as a basis for other cartridges to be made from their brass by modifying different parts of the cartridge (neck width, overall length, etc.). This process is called "wildcatting." That is, unless it is done by a gun manufacturer or ammunition maker. Then it's called "product development."

Cartridges that were based on longer bullets, such as the .30-06 or .25-06, are described as "long action." This is because the bolt must be pulled back farther in order for the ejected shell to clear the chamber. As new cartridges were developed from shorter cartridges such as the .308 Winchester, or the "Short Magnum" series of cartridges, a much shorter travel distance was required. Subsequently, this drove the development of rifles that were custom designed for this class of cartridge.

A Note on Military Surplus Bolt Actions

Many armies of the world used bolt-action rifles for lots of years. Recently, a flood of surplus rifles have been hitting the used gun market. Many of these have come from the former communist countries who are looking for hard currency. Most of these guns make excellent shooters. It can be a real thrill to own and shoot a rifle that may have actually seen action in some of the pivotal battles of WWII. British Short Magazine Lee Enfield (SMLE) Mark III and Mark IV rifles; Russian Mosin-Nagant M91/30 rifles (and M38 and M44 carbines); German, Croatian, and Turkish Mausers; Italian Carcanos, Swiss Schmidt-Rubin K31 rifles, and more can be had for around $100. While rough, these make excellent collector pieces, "plinkers," and hunting rifles. In addition to the rifles, a great deal of surplus ammunition has come in with the rifles, making them very affordable to shoot.

SemiAutomatic Rifles

As we learned in the handgun chapter, "semiautomatic" means that as the shooter pulls the trigger, a single round is fired, and the chamber is emptied and reloaded. Pulling the trigger again repeats the process until the magazine is empty. Just like the pistols we discussed earlier, there are also semiautomatic rifles and carbines. The semiautomatic rifle development was spurred by military needs to be able to deliver greater firepower in a shorter amount of time. Civilians too enjoyed the ability to have fast follow-up shots for target shooting/plinking, or hunting.

Most semiautomatic rifles work by using the escaping gas from the bullet exiting the barrel to operate the action, or use the inertia from the recoil of the round being fired to operate the action. Since part of the recoil force is used to operate the action, most semiautomatic rifles have less recoil than their bolt, pump, or lever-action brethren.

Having the ability to fire rapidly means that the semiautomatic must also have an internal magazine to provide ammunition. This is not so much an advantage for hunting as it is for plinking, personal protection, and some competitions. Magazines can take several forms. For smaller-caliber weapons such as .17-caliber HMR and H2, and .22s, a tubular magazine works fine (but is slow to reload). In larger guns such as the Ruger Ranch Rifle, Mini-14, and surplus military arms such as the AR 15, FAL, AK-47, an external magazine is typically used. Some "transitional model" semiautomatics such as the Russian SKS, used an internal ten-round magazine that was loaded from the top of the rifle.

SKS with stripper clip inserted

Please be aware that civilian shooters may not own *fully automatic* weapons without special licenses and extensive background checks. As a result, even though you can buy an AK-47, it is the civilian "semiautomatic" version of the weapon. This is a great time to pause and talk about the "evil assault rifle."

The Evil Assault Rifle

The typical bolt-action rifle that was in use in the Second World War fired five rounds was about fifty meters long and weighed eight to nine pounds. That's a lot of weight to schlep around for only five shots! The cartridges these rifles fired were powerful, and not a lot of fun to learn how to shoot accurately. These cartridges were made to shoot long distances. If you look at most military rifles, their sights are set for up to two thousand yards.

Military studies and focus group revealed that most troops didn't need that kind of power, because the enemy was seldom shot at over three hundred yards. Late in WWII, the Germans developed the first weapon that was light-weight, fired from a magazine, was fully automatic, and had a lower-powered round that didn't beat up the soldier's shoulder. The eloquent, romantic devils that they are, the German military named the rifle the "Sturmgewher," which translates as "storm rifle," which became loosely translated as "assault rifle."

Picture of Sturmgewher rifle from Wikipedia site

With the fall of Communism and the expansion of Chinese capitalism, a flood of *semiautomatic* versions of these military-style rifles came into the country. Due to their "catchy name" and their military appearance, they were instantly vilified as "weapons of criminals" instead of collectables, plinkers, and even hunting rifles. The appearance of the assault rifle came to galvanize the "antigun" camp and as part of the Brady Bill, the importation and manufacture of new assault guns was cut back for ten years. All this really accomplished was to drive up the price of the existing weapons already in the sales channel and in the hands of private citizens. The "progun" camp argued that since all these weapons were semiautomatic, and the definition of an assault rifle was that it was "fully automatic," *none* of the rifles being identified by "the antis" should be banned. Since the Brady Bill has now expired and has not been reenacted, it looks like the "progun" camp was right after all.

Pump-Action Rifles

Pump-action rifles represent a small niche in any review of firearms, but are significant. The first pump action rifles were introduced by Colt (the *Colt Lightning*) to rival Winchester's dominance in the rifle arena. Colt soon dropped production based on the finicky nature of their design and the threat from Winchester that they might just go into the handgun business. The first mainstream pump action rifles were small .22 rimfire guns that were popular in shooting galleries across the United States. Many of these guns were made by Winchester, although many "store brands" were also offered under the "Sears," "Western Auto," and "Belknap" names.

Most pump-action rifles have a tubular magazine. Rounds are first loaded into the magazine. Then a rearward motion of the forearm readies a round to be loaded into the chamber. Moving the forearm forward completes the loading and the gun is ready to fire. After firing, moving the forearm to the rear extracts the spent cartridge and the process is repeated. Because the shooter's hands never have to change position on the gun, pump-action rifles are a real (pardon the pun) *blast* to shoot. Many Coke cans have met their untimely end at the business end of a Winchester Model 65, a Henry H003, or a Taurus model 62.

Restrictive gun laws in some countries (namely Australia) and interest in Cowboy Action Shooting/historical firearms collecting have rekindled an interest in the reintroduction of the Colt Lightning rifle. Beretta (and some of its subsidiaries and importers), American Western Arms, and Taurus all make a replica of the famous Colt rifle. Remington, Savage, Sauer, and Browning currently make a slide (or pump) action centerfire rifle that is chambered in calibers suitable for big game. Interestingly, the Remington product offering is being marketed to law enforcement since most officers are already familiar with its operation (which is identical to the Remington 870 pump-action shotgun).

Remington 7615 Police Model

Single-Shot Rifles

Naturally, the first rifles were single-shot rifles. In a rare move of thriftiness on the part of the U.S. government, the first cartridge rifle that saw widespread deployment with our troops was created by cutting the back off of a Springfield percussion cap rifle, and installing a hinged cover with a spring-loaded release. The solider would pull back on a hammer, press the release (which would spring open the cover), and load a single cartridge. The rifle could then be fired and the process repeated. These rifles were known as "Trapdoor Springfields" and some are still being shot today! Other famous rifles of the post–Civil War period are still being produced (although *reproduced* would be a much more appropriate term). The famous Sharps rifle, Ballard, Winchester High Wall, Low Wall, Falling Block, Remington Rolling Block can be purchased in calibers from .22 rimfire up to the booming loads like .45-70, .45-90, and 50-caliber rounds.

Most of these rifles are used for an exciting shooting discipline called Black Powder Cartridge Rifle (or BPCR). Shooters load cartridges that were popular in the late 1800s with real black powder (or modern substitutes) and shoot at long ranges at steel silhouette cutouts of chickens, pigs, turkeys, and rams.

History aside, there are still many single-shot rifles made today. Many of these are made to wring extreme accuracy out of a rifle, either for competition or for hunting. Some hunters like the challenge or hunting with only one round in the chamber. For others, legal restrictions on the number of rounds in the gun come into play. Ruger, Marlin/Harrington & Richardson, Taylor & Company, EMF Company all make modern single-shot rifles with actions that will withstand modern, smokeless loads (always consult the owner's manual before firing any load).

The Chipmunk

Many people will ask, "What is the best rifle to start a child shooting?" Naturally, you can now see that there is no "holy grail" of firearms that is the "right gun" for everyone. One firearm that should get special mention is the Rogue Rifle Company's Chipmunk. The Chipmunk is a "single-shot bolt action," .22 rimfire rifle that is scaled down for small shooters. In fact the whole rifle only measures thirty inches and weighs in at two and a half pounds! Since this gun is a single shot, it stresses safety and focuses the new shooter on making that one shot count.

Black-Powder Rifles

Modern black-powder rifles were created to address the needs of hunters wishing to take advantage of "primitive weapon hunting seasons" in their states, but who wanted more performance than what was offered by 19th-century reproduction firearms.

These guns still use the black powder formula or modern synthetic black powder (which is less corrosive than true black powder) and an external source of ignition (such as a shotgun primer or percussion cap). This is about where the similarity ends to their similarity to 19th-century weapon.

These modern black powder rifles can mount scopes and other optical sighting devices, can be had with synthetic stocks, and can even be totally camouflaged. Leaders in this field are Connecticut Valley Arms (CVA), Thompson Center, Traditions, and Knight.

Due to the nature of firearms regulations at the writing of this book, no background check is required to purchase or own a black powder weapon, but it sure wouldn't be my first choice for a home defense firearm. These firearms are best left for hunters, and those who enjoy a "link to the past."

Shotguns

After handguns and rifles, the third major class of firearm is the shotgun. The outward appearance of a shotgun is very similar to a rifle. In fact, there are many of the same type of shotgun actions as there are rifles (single shot, semiautomatic, pump, even bolt, and lever-action). The chief difference is that a rifle fires a single projectile at a time, a shotgun can fire one or several hundred at a time.

Shotguns were some of the first firearms developed. Prior to the invention of rifling, it was common to load several smaller balls into the shooters musket to go after spread-out, quick-moving game like waterfowl, rabbits, and squirrels.

Modern shotguns use shells to hold the load of projectiles that the gun will fire. These consist of the shell (a brass and plastic container), a primer, a powder charge, a wad, and the shot or slug.

What Does "Gauge" Mean?

Shotguns are grouped by the diameter of their barrels (not calibers like rifles and handguns). The standard measure of this is "gauge" ("gage" is an alternate spelling and perfectly acceptable). The term came about as a way to standardize the products that gunsmiths were turning out in the days before shells (when shotguns were loaded from the muzzle and used flintlocks to ignite the powder). So to test the "gauge" of a shotgun, you filled the bore with steel balls the diameter of the bore. The number of balls it took to reach one pound of shot was the "gauge." The most common gauge in use

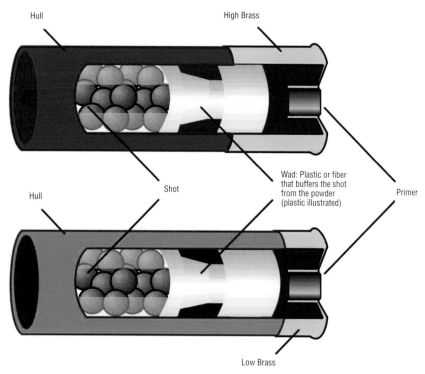

A twelve-gauge shotgun shell in a translucent plastic hull, showing the contents. From right to left: primer, powder, wad, shot, and the hull

today is the twelve-gauge. Other factory-produced gauges include the 10, 12, 16, 20, 28, and .410. You'll notice that at the small end, the diminutive .410 is a decimal number. That is because the .410 is the exception to the rule. The .410 is the inside diameter of that particular shotgun's bore and not its gauge. That is because the .410 is a relative newcomer to the shotgun family, being invented for the game of skeet. Just for grins, it would be about a sixty-seven–gauge if you were to figure it that way.

So what is a shotgun used for?

In the beginning of this book we listed four main purposes for a firearm: (1) personal defense, (2) personal accomplishment/fun/plinking, (3) hunting, and/or (4) collecting. Shotguns can easily fill each of these

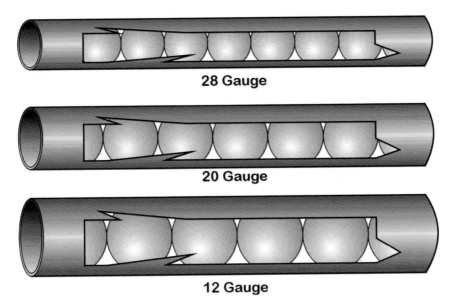

28 Gauge

20 Gauge

12 Gauge

Illustration of how "gauge" is measured

needs, although, like the handguns and rifles we've studied previously, seldom can one shotgun fit all needs.

Many of the finer shotguns are then "graded" within that type. Various "grades" indicate the level of detail engraving, extra fancy wood stocks, and/or inlays of precious metals. Modern shotguns are typically separated by their action type. Therefore, the best way to examine the shotgun is to look at each of the actions and then to examine their uses.

Double Barrel

The double-barrel shotgun conjures up two images for me. The first is the "upper-class society" out for a spot of hunting before tea. The second is the trusty companion of the stagecoach driver in the old west fending off "bad guys." So both images are overly dramatic, but they do tend to describe the modern use of the double-barrel shotgun.

Double-barrel shotguns today are mainly used in hunting birds (and other small animals like rabbits and squirrels), and in the sport of Cowboy

Action Shooting, although, their simple nature makes them an effective personal defense choice as well. Many of the finer double shotguns such as Purdy, Fox, and Holland & Holland (to name a few) can fetch prices in the $30,000 range, so the collectable nature of these fine guns can not be overlooked.

Hammers versus Hammerless

Double barrels are also known as "side by side," or abbreviated as "SxS." They are further grouped by the presence of external cocking hammers versus internal hammers. Over the years, internal hammer firearms have picked up the name "hammerless"; however, they really do have hammers, just not on the outside.

CZ Ringneck hammerless double barrel—note single trigger

So hammered or hammerless double? It depends on your application. Hammered double shotguns were the first made. Within a few years, hammerless doubles hit the market. Hammered guns continued to be made and offered as a product differentiator. Several replica versions of hammered shotguns pop up from time to time from places like Brazil, Turkey, and China; however, these guns are typically targeted toward the "Old West collector and shooting market." The most prolific maker of these is IAC from China, who import the handy IAC Model 99 Coach Gun.

Today, most double barrels that are still offered are hammerless. Stevens, Stoeger, Ruger, Charles Daly, KBI, Baikal, and many more offer double barrel shotguns. Typically these guns are best suited for hunting situations where a fast follow-up shot is required, or for Cowboy Action Shooting.

IAC Model 99 hammered double barrel

One Trigger or Two?

Another consideration for both a double barrel or an over/under shotgun is the number of triggers. Original guns had two triggers—one for each barrel—so that each barrel could be fired independently. Newer innovations have resulted in some shotguns coming with a single trigger that is reset to fire the second barrel by the recoil of the first shot. Furthermore, a selector is added to set which barrel is fired by the first shot. It's really the shooter's preference. Some swear that having to only memorize where the single trigger is located is easier than memorizing the location of two triggers. Others swear by the reliability of two triggers.

Single-trigger guns are often used in the sports of trap or skeet where the second barrel may be chambered with a different "choke" than the first.

Pump

Think back to every movie and TV show you've ever seen. Someone is carrying a shotgun and pumps a shell into the chamber and your blood turns a little colder. This is because Hollywood has trained us to instantly recognize the sound of a pump shotgun action. Oddly enough, the more you watch, the more you'll realize that these "heroes" and "villains" are usually moving or "racking" the slide unnecessarily! Watch, I'm not making this up! They will pump the action to load a round into the chamber. At that point, the shotgun is ready to fire. Typically, they will then go sneaking around the "bad guys" hideout. Right before they shoot, they'll rack the slide again (thus ejecting a perfectly good, live round), so the "bad guy" can hear it and turn around ("good guys" can't shoot someone in the back) but hey, that's Hollywood.

The pump shotgun was developed in the late 1890s. Both Marlin and Winchester came out with pump action shotguns about the same time (Winchester's hit the streets first and was more famous). Early pump-action shotguns were very complicated affairs and prone to jams and breakages. By the early 20th century all the kinks had been worked out and the pump shotgun has been a perennial favorite of firearms users ever since.

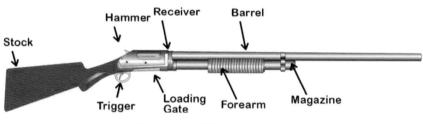

Winchester 1897 pump shotgun

Just like a pump action rifle, the pump action shotgun works by the user manipulating the shotgun's forearm to release a shell from the spring-loaded magazine. Moving the forearm forward causes the lifter to raise the shell as the bolt pushes it into the chamber. The shotgun is now ready for firing. After firing, the user pulls back on the forearm and the extractor pulls the empty shell from the chamber and the ejector throws the round clear of the action as the process repeats itself.

Pump-action shotguns are some of the most versatile of the shotgun family. They are used by the military, police, and civilians as potent weapons for defense, they make great hunting pieces due to their rugged and reliable actions, and their relatively low price makes them an attractive choice for competition guns. While not as collectable as other shotguns, Winchester

1897 shotguns continue to fetch astounding prices due to the popularity of Cowboy Action Shooting.

Pump Guns for Defense

Face it. No matter how much you may or may not know about guns, nothing else sounds like a pump action shotgun being pumped. This can work to the advantage of the homeowner when something goes "bump in the night." There have been many documented cases where the simple sound of a shotgun being loaded sent an unseen intruder fleeing a house. Pump action shotguns are a fine choice for home defense, especially if you have a long hallway. Care must be exercised in the use of these shotguns inside. When loaded with slugs or buckshot, pump action shotguns have the ability to penetrate walls and kill innocent people. This is another compelling reason to get training if you intend to keep such a weapon in your bedroom (by the way, don't put it under your bed, it'll just get dusty and rusty). If you do keep a shotgun in the home for defense, you might consider loading some number 4 or number 6 birdshot as the first two loads. These loads can kill at close distances, but won't overpenetrate walls. Examples of shotguns that make good choices for personal defense are the Remington 870, the Mossberg 500, Winchester Defender, or even some of the replica arms from China such as the IAC replica of the Winchester 97 or 97 Trench Gun. Barrels should be shorter than twenty inches for personal defense applications. This keeps a potential intruder from grabbing the barrel as you round a corner using leverage to keep you from bringing the gun to bear on target.

Interstate Arms Corporation copy of Remington 870 shotgun. Note rifle sights

Combo Models

Some manufacturers offer interchangeable, two-barrel "sets" that include both a short personal defense barrel and a longer twenty-eight-inch barrel that can be used for hunting and sport shooting (skeet, trap, sporting clays). Over the years Mossberg and its value line Maverick have released several different combinations (wood/synthetic, standard stock/pistol grip, etc).

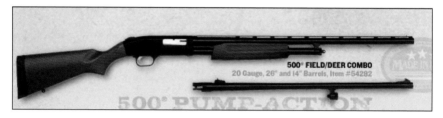

Mossberg Model 500 Field/Deer Combo

Semiautomatic Shotguns

Just as the semiautomatic rifle revolutionized combat, the same principle was soon applied to the shotgun. The chief reason to apply Semiautomatic action to a shotgun is to reduce the recoil from stronger loads. Semiautomatic shotguns function in one of two different ways, "gas operation" or "recoil/inertia operation."

Gas operation traps some of the escaping gases from the shot column, leaving the barrel to work the action (extract/eject the shell, move the bolt, place a round from the magazine on the carrier, lift the shell to the returning bolt, and load it into the chamber). The problem is that there are a wide variety of shotgun shells. Low-velocity rounds that are used for clay target games don't have the same force as loads that are expected to take down geese at altitude. Therefore most gas-operated shotguns have a regulation system. Many of the better ones have a "self-regulating gas system." Examples of gas-operated semiautomatic shotguns include the

SemiAutomatic, Charles Daly, VR-MC in RealTree™ Hardwoods camouflage

Remington 1100, Winchester 1400, Berretta Xtremea2, Charles Daly Field Hunter VR,

The second major type of semiautomatic shotguns are the "recoil"- or "inertia"-operated actions. These shotguns use the force of the recoil (or inertia) to cycle the action. Since they don't rely on gas (which is variable), virtually all shells will cycle an inertia-based semiautomatic without any modification. Recoil-operated shotguns do tend to cost slightly more than gas-operated shotguns. Examples of recoil-operated semiautomatic shotguns include the Franchi I-12 (pronounced "Frank-E"), the Benelli Super Black Eagle II.

Semiautomatic shotguns can be used for most any application; however, they do tend to be more expensive than pump action shotguns. As a result, police and military agencies have been slow to adopt them for security and personal defense applications. As a result, there are very few semiautomatic shotguns that are available from the factory with short barrels.

Over/Under

The "over/under" shotgun is a relative newcomer to the family of shotguns, dating back to the 1930s. As the name implies, the over/under shotgun features two barrels, stacked one on top of the other. Over/under shotguns are usually abbreviated as "o/u" or referred to as "stacked barrels," or by the first trade name, "superposed."

The O/U was first introduced by Browning and was designed to provide hunters and skeet shooters a quick second shot at game or clay targets. While a Double Barrel shotgun provided much the same functionality, it does not provide the same sight picture as the shooter swings through the arc of the shot as two barrels, one on top of the other. The O/U was not an instant hit (poor timing due to it being introduced at the beginning of the Great Depression). The popularity was increased by World War II. Thousands of bomber crews were taught aerial gunning skills by shooting skeet targets from the back of moving trucks. After the war, sales increased as the veterans returned home (with money in their pockets).

While a natural for hunting, many O/U are also employed for sport and recreational shooting. They are very popular for skeet, trap, and sporting clays.

To shoot skeet, four gauges are used: 12, 20, 28, and .410. Many O/U shotguns are offered as "four-barreled sets" where the owner has one stock and receiver and simply changes out the barrels. An alternative to this is to have "sleeves" that screw into the twelve-gauge barrels that reduce the inside diameter for the smaller-diameter shells.

Engraved Ruger Red Label 12-gauge O/U shotgun

Until recently, O/U shotguns were *very* expensive. It was very difficult to get into an O/U for less than $1,500. This is still a valid benchmark for most of the "big names" in O/U shoguns, with prices for four-barreled sets escalating from there. It is not uncommon for a serious competitor to pay $25,000–$30,000 for a fine, four-barreled O/U. In addition to Browning, makers include Ruger, Krieghoff, Beretta.

Fortunately, for those of less means, many serviceable O/U shotguns are being imported from Brazil, Russia, and Turkey under the Stoeger, Baikal, CZ-USA, and Charles Daly brands for well under $700.

As a side note to the O/U, it is important to mention the drilling. Drillings were a class of weapon that originated in Germany and combined one or more rifle barrels with a shotgun barrel. The idea was that you'd be ready no matter what kind of game was encountered. A few specialty companies still offer these combination guns. Savage made an excellent one that the user could choose from several different choices of the rifle and shotgun. Still offered today is the Springfield Armory M6. This handy little weapon featured a .22 rifle barrel (or a .22 Magnum version was available) and a .410 shotgun. The gun was intended chiefly for backpackers and other outdoorsmen as a light way to pack into the wilderness.

Specialty/Novelty/Lever-action/Bolt Action

This section could just as easily be described as *"other."* Shotguns have been around for a *long* time. There have been lots of different types of developments.

Historically, one of the first "repeater" shotguns was the Winchester Model 1887. Winchester wanted to offer a "repeating" shotgun to build on their line of repeating rifles. Since their rifles used a "lever-action," Oliver Winchester asked John Browning to design a twelve-gauge shotgun based on the lever-action principle. Browning was less than thrilled with the project, but the money was good. Browning, by the way, thought that the "pump" action would be better and went on to prove it by designing the 1893 (and later the improved 1897) designs, which he then also sold to Winchester.

One of the most unique shotguns available today is the "Snake Charmer" from Verney-Carron USA. This shotgun is offered in .410 gauge (the smallest shotgun gauge) and is billed as an ideal firearm for personal protection while doing yard work or backpacking. That's not a hard claim to support. At twenty-nine inches and about four pounds, the Snake Charmer is very unobtrusive shotgun, and its .410 shell is very effective against snakes, wild dogs, and other "varmints" (raccoons, opossums, etc.).

Also in this category are .410 revolvers! Taurus currently offers the model 4410 Tracker, a five-shot .410 *handgun*. This gun is instantly recognizable by its almost three-inch long cylinder. An additional advantage of this setup is that this handgun can also fire .45 Long Colt rounds. This makes it a potentially interesting option for personal protection on a ranch where you may encounter both snakes and larger threats.

Another interesting shotgun is the Winchester Model 1887. This shotgun was also designed by John Browning at Winchester's request. In the 1880s, Winchester desired to market a repeating shotgun to match its repeating rifle. Originals of the 1887 and the improved 1901 fetch handsome amounts of money on the collectors' markets. It is not unusual to see them priced at over $1,000. Fortunately, shooters may elect to purchase affordable replica versions from IAC. Movie fans might recognize the 1887 as the shotgun that Arnold Schwarzenegger uses in the *Terminator II* movie and Brendan Frazier uses in *The Mummy's Return*.

Another interesting type of shotgun is the bolt-action shotgun. These guns were made by Marlin, primarily for waterfowl hunting. They fed from

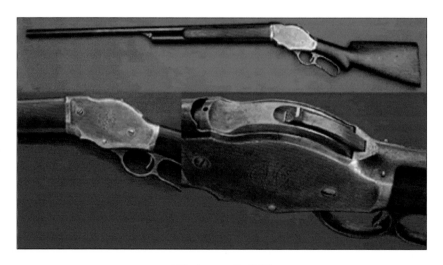

Winchester M 1887

a detachable magazine in the stock. It is rare that one might come across a bolt-action shotgun.

Single-Barrel Shotgun

Another choice for a shotgun is the single-barrel. These shotguns typically fall into two categories: entry-level or high-level competition guns. At the "entry level," several firms offer a single-barrel shotgun for around $100. These guns are best used to instruct new shooters in shotgun safety (since they only fire one round at a time). It should be noted that recoil from these guns can be brutal, and aftermarket slip-on recoil pads and/or shoulder pads should be worn. While these guns may be used for personal defense, it's not recommended due to their stout recoil and lack of a second shot. The other class of single-shot shotguns are made primarily for trap shooting. These guns are specifically balanced and choked to shoot the game of trap and usually start around $1,500.

A Note on Choke

A shotgun's "choke" is a narrowing or constriction of the barrel at the end (or muzzle). This constriction helps pull the shot column together as it exits the barrel. The result is how the shot hits the target. The measure of how a shot hits a target is called its pattern. By varying the choke in a shotgun, you adjust not only how tight the pattern is but at what distance. A "full choke" will hold the shot together for the longest distance. A "modified choke" is optimized for close work while an "improved modified" is good for medium distances on clay birds or small game (such as quail). Other chokes are specialized for turkey hunting or skeet shooting.

Another aspect of choke is the effect it has on recoil. Shotguns are famous for having stout recoil. Choke plays a significant part in the recoil of a shotgun. This dissuades many shooters from even trying shotguns. Since the shot column is being restricted as it exits the barrel, more force is felt by the shooter (Newton's third law). There are several strategies for dealing with this additional recoil. The first of which is taking lessons in the proper way to mount and shoot a shotgun. Stance has a lot to do with making

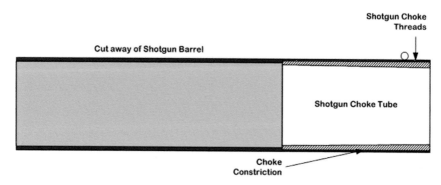

A screw-in type shotgun choke

shotgunning enjoyable. On a more tangible note, mercury-filled pistons (marked under the name "Dead Mules" and recoil-operated devices, even filling the stock with additional weight, can counter recoil. Another process is to *"backbore"* the shotgun's barrel(s). Backboring provides a more gradual constriction of the barrel into the chokes and eases recoil.

Shotgun chokes are typically set in one of two ways. The first is that the barrel is factory cut to have a single choke. These are the least expensive shotguns, but also the least useful. This is because in order to change the choke, you must change the whole barrel, and replacement barrels can run up to $100 each. The second most common method of applying choke is by a "choke tube" that screws into the end of the barrel. Choke tubes must be matched to the thread diameter of the individual manufacturer. For example, it would not be wise to screw a Mossberg choke into a Remington barrel. Choke tubes usually run $20–$30 each.

CHAPTER

4

How Do I Choose Which Gun to Buy?

At this point, you should have a pretty good idea what you might want to buy a gun for and what tasks might match which type of gun. Now is the hard part . . . deciding which one to buy.

This chapter will help guide you through the process of selecting which gun you might like to buy. Remember, you won't be "married" to this gun. If you buy it and you end up not liking it, you can just sell it to someone else. Some stores may even let you trade the gun in for store credit, but you won't make near what you've got in the gun that way.

The trick is to listen to the sales staff. They will help you select the right firearm for your needs if you let them. Whenever possible, try before you buy.

Gun Shop Etiquette

Ah, you've made it into the gun store, sporting goods gun counter, or gun show. You've made it up to the counter, and the helpful attendant asks how they can help. You indicate that you'd like to see the Smith & Wesson Sigma semiautomatic pistol in the case.

At this point, there are a few points of etiquette that should be observed. Following these guidelines will identify you to the salesperson as someone who is to be trusted with a gun and taken seriously. It's just human nature.

Rule 1 – Never point the gun at a person. "No one is ever shot with a loaded gun." It is always the "I thought it was an empty gun" that shoots someone. Remember commandment 1 from the gun owners' ten commandments: Treat every gun as if it were loaded. And in doing so, that means don't point it at someone even if it's empty.

If you point a gun at the salesperson, will they get mad at you and throw you out? Most likely not. They want to sell you a gun and most are "used" to having guns pointed at them; however, no one is ever "comfortable" with having a gun pointed at them.

Rule 2 – Always check to make sure the weapon is empty. Typically, when you ask to see the gun, the clerk will pick up the gun, point the muzzle in a safe direction, and open the firearm's action to make sure that the weapon is unloaded. They will then hand you the gun. *Never* accept a gun from someone without checking the action *yourself*. As soon as you take possession of the firearm, open it up. Visually inspect the chamber to make darn sure that there are no rounds in the magazine. Close the chamber and continue your inspection.

Rule 3 – Always ask the salesperson if it is permissible to "dry fire" the gun. An important way to check the action of a gun is to pull the trigger through its cycle (single-action or double-action) with the chambers empty. This is usually OK for a limited number of times. This doesn't mean that you should snap away a hundred times. Two to three should be sufficient to get the feel of the trigger. Also, dry firing a rimfire gun can damage both the gun and the hammer. This practice should be discouraged for .22- and .17-caliber rimfire guns.

Rule 4 – Well, more of a guideline. Most stores may only show you one gun at a time. Some will show you up to two so that you can size up one against another. This is done for security and loss prevention. Don't ask to see more than two guns at a time.

Rule 5 – Listen to what the salesperson has to say. It's their job to sell you the right firearm for your needs. If you feel like you are being snowballed or rushed, thank the person for their time and try somewhere else.

Rule 6 – Do not disassemble the gun (even if you know how). That is usually not a requirement for buying a gun, and you run the risk of losing a critical piece.

Rule 7 – Try to be considerate of the salesperson's time. Most gun store salesperson work for wage and a small commission on the guns that they sell. Even though you may be buying a $400–$700 handgun, that may only mean $20 in their pocket. If someone else is in the store and they look like they want to buy something immediately, let the salesperson go wait on them while you think about it and look at the guns. The salesperson wants to get you the right gun, but they need to eat too.

Gun Shows

Gun shows are a terrific way to see a *lot* of guns in a short period of time. A gun show is an event (usually organized by a promoter, just like a rock concert) where vendors rent tables to sell their products to consumers. After the Columbine tragedy, gun shows received a lot of bad press because the children involved and the dealer involved broke the law. He sold guns to minors. You don't see this much at gun shows. Most vendors are honorable men and women just looking for a legal venue to sell their product to a larger audience. "If you can't bring Mohammed to the mountain, bring the mountain to Mohammed." Remember, the same rules that apply to a gun store apply to a gun show.

Typically, there is a "door charge" that goes to the promoter. After you pay that charge, there is usually a "security checkpoint" where guns that are being brought to sell are checked and have their actions secured. Most will not permit you to carry loose ammo or loaded magazines. Don't give the nice policemen a hard time! Having a concealed carry permit means nothing, as most would not permit you to carry in a public gathering anyway.

I always try to tour the entire show before I buy anything. That is, unless you find "the deal of the century," then go with your gut instinct. Depending on local laws, there can be two types of dealers at these shows: federally licensed dealers and private sales dealers. Licensed dealers are usually the owners of gun stores who are bringing inventory to sell. They possess a Federal Firearms License or FFL to sell guns and must follow all federal, state, and local laws. Private sales dealers are individuals who buy a table to sell their guns. Since they are not federal dealers, there is no requirement for them to fill out any paperwork or perform any background checks. It's just one citizen selling a widget to another citizen. In most states, *this is perfectly legal.*

Finally, gun shows are notorious for being cramped. Please try to be polite. Remember, most of those people have guns.

Try Before You Buy

Most larger cities have indoor gun ranges. Many outdoor gun ranges have a "range store" attached. In many of these places, you can "rent" a gun for use at the range. This is the *best* way to buy a gun. You've narrowed down your choices to two to three guns. Go rent them at the range and try them out. Often you can "rent" a gun for as little as $5 a session. Some ranges will even let you "trade it back" and try something else. Most "rental" guns require that you use ammunition provided by the range. This is to protect their investment in the firearms against people who load their own ammunition.

For most ranges you simply have to show up, fill out a waiver, have eye and ear protection. You'll usually be asked to purchase your targets at the range. Most often you'll be assigned a shooting position. When you get to the position, there is often an individual light to light your area. Clip your target to the holder and use the pulley (or electronic switch) to move the target "downrange." You may then load your firearm and start shooting.

If you are shooting a handgun, try it at about seven yards first. When you can comfortably keep all your shots within a four-inch to five-inch area, feel free to move the target back. Remember, to become proficient at shooting takes thousands or repetitions. Very few of us are "Tiger Woods" the first time we step out onto the golf course.

Indoor ranges are very expensive to build and insure. Please follow all safety guidelines.

Completing the Sale

When you have made your decision to buy a particular firearm from a dealer, you'll have to start "the paperwork." That means that you'll be given a pen and a copy of BATFE[8] form 4473 (see sample below). This form is retained by the dealer. U.S. law forbids the entry of this data into *any* database.

Once the paperwork has been completed, the dealer will call the Instant Check System to perform a background check on the buyer. Often this is accomplished in just a few minutes; however, call volume during peak hours often results in delays. Your dealer cannot give you possession of the firearm until he is given an authorization code from Instant Check. Don't be surprised if you cannot leave the dealer with your gun. It make take a few minutes to a day. In many states, a valid concealed carry permit/license will serve as the background check, and the dealer will not have to make the call to Instant Check.

---

8 Bureau of Alcohol, Tobacco, Firearms, and Explosives

U.S. Department of Justice
Bureau of Alcohol, Tobacco, Firearms and Explosives

OMB No. 1140-0020

Firearms Transaction Record Part I -
Over-the-Counter

WARNING: You may not receive a firearm if prohibited by Federal or State Law. The information you provide will be used to determine whether you are prohibited under law from receiving a firearm. Certain violations of the Gun Control Act are punishable by up to 10 years imprisonment and/or up to a $250,000 fine.

Transferor's Transaction Serial Number

Prepare in original only. All entries must be in ink. Read the Important Notices, Instructions and Definitions on this form. "Please Print."

Section A - Must Be Completed Personally By Transferee (Buyer)

1. Transferee's Full Name

Last Name	First Name	Middle Name *(If no middle name state "NMN")*

2. Current Residence Address **(Cannot be a post office box.)**

Number and Street Address	City	County	State	Zip Code

3. Place of Birth

U.S. City/State   Foreign Country

4. Height   Ft. _____   In. _____

5. Weight

6. Gender   Male ☐   Female ☐

7. Birth Date   Month   Day   Year

8. Social Security Number *(Optional, but will help prevent misidentification.)*

9. Unique Personal Identification Number *(UPIN)* if applicable *(See Instruction to Transferor 6.)*

10. Race *(Ethnicity) (Check one or more boxes.)*

☐ American Indian or Alaska Native   ☐ Black or African American   ☐ Native Hawaiian or Other Pacific Islander
☐ Hispanic or Latino   ☐ Asian   ☐ White

11. Answer questions 11.a. through 12 by writing **"yes"** or **"no"** in the boxes to the right of the questions.

a. Are you the actual buyer of the firearm(s) listed on this form? **Warning: You are not the actual buyer if you are acquiring the firearm(s) on behalf of another person. If you are not the actual buyer, the dealer cannot transfer the firearm(s) to you.** *(See Important Notice 1 for actual buyer definition and examples.)*

b. Are you under indictment or information in any court for a **felony**, or any other crime, for which the judge could imprison you for more than one year? *(An information is a formal accusation of a crime by a prosecutor. See Definition 3.)*

c. Have you ever been convicted in any court of a **felony**, or any other crime, for which the judge could have imprisoned you for more than one year, even if you received a shorter sentence including probation? *(See Important Notice 4, Exception 1.)*

d. Are you a fugitive from justice?

e. Are you an unlawful user of, or addicted to, marijuana, or any depressant, stimulant, or narcotic drug, or any other controlled substance?

f. Have you ever been adjudicated mentally defective *(which includes having been adjudicated incompetent to manage your own affairs)* or have you ever been committed to a mental institution?

g. Have you been discharged from the Armed Forces under **dishonorable** conditions?

h. Are you subject to a court order restraining you from harassing, stalking, or threatening your child or an intimate partner or child of such partner? *(See Important Notice 5.)*

i. Have you ever been convicted in any court of a misdemeanor crime of domestic violence? *(See Important Notice 4, Exception 1 and Definition 4.)*

j. Have you ever renounced your United States citizenship?

k. Are you an alien **illegally** in the United States?

l. Are you a nonimmigrant alien? *(See Definition 6.) If you answered "no" to this question, you are not required to respond to question 12.*

12. If you answered "yes" to question 11.l., do you fall within any of the exceptions set forth in Important Notice 4, Exception 2? (e.g., valid State hunting license.) **(If "yes," the licensee must complete question 20c.)**

13. What is your State of residence *(if any)?* _____ *(See Definition 5. If you are not a citizen of the United States, you only have a State of residence if you have resided in a State for at least 90 continuous days immediately prior to the date of this sale.)*

14. What is your country of citizenship? *(List/check more than one, if applicable.)*
☐ United States of America   ☐ Other *(Specify)* _____

15. If you are not a citizen of the United States, what is your U.S.-issued alien number or admission number? _____

Note: Previous Editions Are Obsolete

ATF Form 4473 (5300.9) Part I
Revised July 2005

BATFE form 4473

CHAPTER

5

Ammunition *or* FMJ – LRN – M-O-U-S-E

Believe it or not, the topic of ammunition selection is the "hard" part of learning about firearms. Why? Well, because there is really no rhyme or reason as to why ammunition is identified. Need some proof? How about this. The following cartridges all have the same bore diameter, about .357": .38 Long Colt, .38 S&W, .38 Colt Police, .38 S&W Special, .357 Magnum, .9 mm Parabellum, .380 ACP (also called 9 mm Kurz). The difference is all in the length or shape of the case. Oddly enough, the 9 x 18mm round isn't really a 9 mm at all. It really measures 9.3 mm and was designed by the Soviets specifically *not* to chamber in .380 caliber weapons.

You will be astounded when you go to look for ammunition for your new firearm. The variety is amazing. There are many hundreds of manufacturers, bullet types, loads, and even packaging options to deal with, even at your local discount store! This section will help you break down some of that lingo and help you find what you want and need (for your specific shooting application).

A SMALL selection of Ammunition

Caliber – Decimal vs. Metric

The first thing that you'll have to find is the correct cartridges or shells for your firearm. Cartridges are typically grouped by size to make it easier for the shopper to locate their caliber. "Caliber" is the diameter of the inside of the barrel (measured at the deepest grove in the rifling). This measurement may be in standard English measurements or in metric. That's how a .357 became the same diameter as 9 mm. There is no real difference between each measurement systems. In fact, consider the 10 mm. After a disastrous shootout in Miami, the FBI was determined to switch to a more powerful semiauto round. Working with several gun and ammunition manufacturers to develop the round and handgun. But the round proved too powerful for service (tending to overpenetrate the target). When Smith & Wesson went back to the proverbial drawing board, they shortened the round *but* used the decimal equivalent of 10 mm, .40 S&W.

Often, when new cartridges are developed by ammunition or gun manufacturers, they will desire to differentiate the loading from other, competing loads. This used to be a much larger problem that it is today. For example, in the late 1800s, the standard police caliber in the United States was .32 caliber. Smith & Wesson created a much improved version of this cartridge and began marketing both the cartridges and guns that fired it as .32 S&W Long. Colt didn't want to mention the name of their largest competitor in their advertising. So the Colt Police Positive revolver was chambered in .32 Colt new police cartridge! Which is *exactly* the same size as a .32 S&W Long.

Metric cartridges are often listed as two numbers. The first is the diameter of the bullet, the second is the length of the cartridge case. This is the 9 x 19 mm, 9 x 17, and 9 x 18, 7.62 x 39 mm etc. Even this isn't foolproof. For example, 9 x19 mm is also known as 9 mm Luger, 9 mm Parabellum, or just "9 mm" by most of the world. 9 x 17 mm is known as ".380 ACP" in the United States and 9 mm Kurz (short) in Germany.

The Magnum

Most people have at least heard of the ammunition term "Magnum." This term has a very interesting history. When the gun industry switched from black powder to smokeless powder, it was discovered that smokeless powder required less volume than black powder. This left a significant portion of empty room inside the case between the bullet and the powder. Curiosity lead people to attempt loading more powder until guns literally exploded.

Smith & Wesson design engineers were experimenting too. What they found was that they could take the .38 special round and increase it's velocity from 700 800 fps[9], where the Magnum is commonly loaded from 1,200 to 1,400 fps. This increase in pressure means that a gun must be strengthened to fire the .357 Magnum cartridge. In order to keep people from accidentally firing the round in a gun that was not strong enough, Smith & Wesson lengthened the cartridge. Therefore if someone tried to insert it into a revolver's cylinder, it would stick out the front and prevent closure (of the cylinder). This leaves us with the term "Magnum." Turns out it was an arbitrary marketing decision. The cartridge is named after a "Magnum" of champagne. The chose the name because it sounded "big."

---

9   Feet Per Second

Bullet Types

When shopping for ammunition, the buyer is bombarded with initials. The most common include FMJ, JHP, LRN, SWC, WC, and JFN, but then you also get some "run-on abbreviations," like LRNFP. All of these describe the shape and composition of the bullet/projectile itself. In describing them, let's take a look at bullets today.

In the beginning, bullets were cast of lead and then had lubricants applied around their base (to lubricate the bore as they were fired). These bullets were cast out of alloys that were mostly lead but usually had some other trace metals (such as tin and antimony) to increase their hardness. Many shooters cast their own bullets and reloaded their brass cartridge cases. This was especially true in the early days of cartridge guns when you might not be able run down to the neighborhood Wal-Mart for a box of cartridges. These cartridges are still loaded today. Since lead is a fairly inexpensive metal, and the manufacturing process isn't very complicated, lead ammunition is usually the lowest priced ammunition for a given caliber. Lead bullets were mainly shaped in two ways: "lead rounded nose" (for improved ballistics), "lead rounded nose, flat point" (for use in tubular magazine lever-action rifles). These are designated today as "LRN," and "LRNFP."

Advances in military bullets lead to the creation of the "spitzer"- shaped bullet. This was a long, conical bullet that had much better ballistics than the short, round-nosed bullets of the time. The shape of these bullets make production in lead difficult. The tips got bent or broke off altogether thus decreasing accuracy. This was when the practice of covering the bullet with a stronger metal "skin" or "jacket" was adopted. When this jacket completely encased the lead core, it was known as a "full-metal jacket," or "FMJ."

Another popular type of bullet is the "Wadcutter." These are cylindrically shaped bullets with a flat face that are optimized to make neat holes in targets and are favored by paper-target shooters. The problem with the wadcutter is that they don't feed well in semiautomatic pistols. A wadcutter was developed by forming a bullet like a cone and then bisecting the top of the cone off. These rounds are abbreviated as "semi wadcutter" (or SWC) or "truncated cone wadcutter"(or TCWC). Wadcutters and SWCs are great for training and plinking rounds. One of my favorite "flavors" of ammunition is the Winchester "White Box" load. This is ammunition that is loaded primarily for range and sporting use but is very inexpensive. It is usually sold in FMJ and SWC loads.

In a self-defense scenario, the point of a bullet is to cause such massive damage to the attacker that they stop attacking the victim. The bigger the bullet, the more damage it does. The problem is that at some point, it becomes very inconvenient to carry around a howitzer in one's purse. This is where the hollow-point round comes in. The "hollow-point" round is literally a bullet that has a hole in the center (see illustration). As the round strikes the target, air is trapped in the hollow. The pressure of the round's impact peels the bullet out in the rough form of a mushroom (hence the term "mushrooming") and can make the round almost twice as large. This means that it makes twice the hole and does twice the damage.

Hollow point ammunition—before and after

Some other types of rounds are "hard cast lead" rounds. Hard cast rounds contain other metals alloyed with the lead to make it stronger and less likely to break apart on entering game. These rounds are generally used for hunting large game such as bear, wild boar, moose, and elk. Hard cast rounds are generally identified on the packaging, but not abbreviated. Another type of round that is primarily used for hunting is the "Jacked Flat Point" (or JFP) round. This round is similar to the jacket hollow point, but doesn't have a hole in the end. The jacket tends to keep the round from expanding as it penetrates. These rounds are very useful to hunt wild boar. Rifle hunting rounds that are jacketed but have a rounded, more ballistic profile are referred to as "jacketed soft points", or JSP.

Rifle ammunition has its own nomenclature, but it's similar to handgun ammunition. Rifle ammunition adds the dimension of the base of the bullet to the mix. If the shape of the bullet is rounded in the end, it is referred to as a "boat tail". The effect of the rounded end makes the round tumble upon impact, making a larger wound channel, therefore causing more damage. Boat tail bullets are often abbreviated BT, but usually after the bullet abbreviations, such as 7.62 x 39 JHP BT.

Boat tail bullet

Another type of bullet sometimes encountered for is the gas check. The "gas check" is a small ring of metal (usually copper) that is affixed to the base of the bullet. This ring traps the escaping gases (when the round is fired) and protects the base of the bullet from being deformed. This can improve the stability of the round in flight. When looking at ammunition packages, gas check rounds are usually abbreviated as GC.

In rifle ammunition, the trick is to impart as much velocity to the bullet but still have adequate expansion to cause tissue damage. The Nosler® company solved this problem by adding a plastic tip into their hollow point bullet. The "Ballistic Tip®" permits excellent ballistic performance yet doesn't interfere with expansion once the round has hit its target.

Other Bullet/Ammunition Types

Other bullet and ammunition types are "specials" that one won't (or shouldn't) come across every day. These include CCI shot shells, which are, literally, pistol caliber shotgun shells.

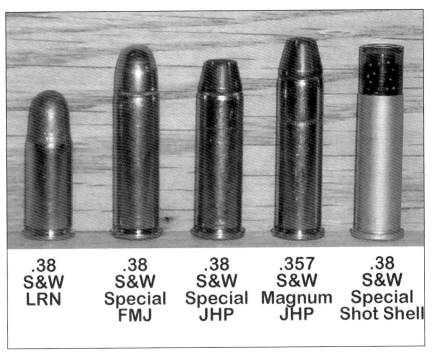

.38
S&W
LRN

.38
S&W
Special
FMJ

.38
S&W
Special
JHP

.357
S&W
Magnum
JHP

.38
S&W
Special
Shot Shell

CCI shot shell (right) shown with other .38/.357 cartridges

Another unique bullet type is the "Glazer Safety Slug." The Glazer Safety Slug consists of a solid jacket around a lead core. The center of the round is filled with small lead pellets and the top is covered with a Teflon cover. Upon impact, most of the round's energy is transferred to the small projectiles. It turns the first object hit into hamburger but won't overpenetrate and kill someone three apartments down. Glazer Safety Slugs are a very good idea for people who live in densely populated areas where overpenetration may be a problem. Be prepared; these rounds are very expensive, usually about $2 each!

Polynomials

No, it isn't a flashback to an Algebra 101 class. Often one will see ammunition that consists of two numbers. Examples would include .44-40, .38-40, .30-30, .45-70, .30-40 Krag, .30-06. I'd like to tell you that there is some logical way to decipher these numbers, but alas, there isn't. In many cases, the first number is the caliber of the round. This is the case for .45-70, and the second number is the charge of black powder used to propel it. This isn't the case for the .38-40 which is a 40-caliber size. Or in the case of the popular .30-30, the first number is the caliber (7.62 mm or .30 caliber) and the second number is the amount of *smokeless* power to load. Then you have the .30-06 (which is pronounced "thirty ought six"). This bullet has an interesting history. It was originally adopted in 1903 as the standard replacement for the underpowered .30-40 Krag. When adopted, the .30-caliber round featured an LNR bullet and was given the nomenclature of .30 (for thirty caliber) dash (-) 03 (for the year of adoption) or .30-03. In 1906, a FMJ, Spitzer boat tail bullet was adopted, and the round was redesignated as .30-06. Your government at work. It is just something that must be memorized on a case-to-case basis.

Shot Shells, Shot, Buckshot, and Slugs

As we've shown earlier, a shotgun fires a shot shell. This shot shell contains one or more projectiles. These projectiles are called "shot." This section decodes shotgun shells.

Early shotgun shells were waxed cardboard. These "paper shells" were prone to water damage, especially in highly humid areas. As a result, brass hulls were adopted and used (by the U.S. Army and Marines) through WWII. In 1960, the first plastic shells were introduced. Like the brass hulls these could be reloaded. Once a shell is fired, the remainder is referred to as a "hull." These can be reloaded several times, but this only makes sense if you shoot a *lot* of shotgun shells. The earliest shells weretwo and a half inches long. Shooters who want to use "Grandpa's old shotgun" should have the piece thoroughly checked out by a gunsmith prior to use. Modern shot shells measure two and three-fourths inches, but three inches and three and a half inches magnum shells are also available. Most modern shotguns plainly mark the maximum length that the shot gun can chamber. *Never try to shoot a shell that exceeds the marked chamber length!* This can lead to serious injury to the shotgun and to the shooter!

Some hulls have a deeper copper base to the shell. This provides additional support for the powder charge. These type of shells are usually referred to as "high brass," as opposed to "low brass." Beware if someone hands you a shot shell that has a half-inch collar instead of the normal one-fourth-inch low brass collar. It might be stronger than you're anticipating.

Birdshot and Buckshot

Shot is usually composed of lead pellets that are of standard size. When this size gets above .24"(or 6 mm) it ceases to be called "birdshot," and is called "buckshot" (meaning that is intended for deer-sized targets). Over the years, the amount of lead in lakes and marshes caused the U.S. Federal government to step in and required "nontoxic" shot to hunt ducks and geese. Acceptable substitutes include shot that is made from steel, tungsten, and bismuth alloys. These metals have different shot characteristics and pattering than lead. Never attempt to shoot steel shot through a barrel or choke type that is not "proofed" (certified) for steel shot.

The table below details shot sizes and the typical number of pellets found in a shell. Note the difference that steel shot has on the number of pellets. This is because steel is lighter than lead.

Birdshot			
Size	Nominal Diameter	Pellets per Ounce	
		Lead	Steel
BBB	.19"(4.83 mm)		62
BB	.18" (4.57 mm)	50	72
1	.16"(4.06 mm)		103
2	.15"(3.81 mm)	87	125
3	.14" (3.56 mm)		158
4	.13" (3.3 mm)	135	192
5	.12" (3.05 mm)	170	243
6	.11"(2.79 mm)	225	315
7½	.095" (2.41 mm)	350	
8	.09" (2.29 mm)	410	
9	.08" (2.03 mm)	585	

Buckshot		
Size	Nominal diameter	Pellets/oz
000 ("triple-ought")	.36" (9.1 mm)	6
00 ("double-ought")	.33" (8.4 mm)	8
0 ("one-ought")	.32" (8.1 mm)	9
1	.30" (7.6 mm)	10
2	.27" (6.9 mm)	15
3	.25" (6.4 mm)	18
4	.24" (6 mm)	21

Which shot size should you buy? If you are just going to shoot targets (clay birds), then size seven and a half, eight, or nine is perfectly acceptable.

These are also good for hunting most birds up to the size of pheasants. For turkey, you should consider something in the range of number 3–6 birdshot. For personal defense situations I favor 00 buckshot. Consider this: a standard load of "double ought" buckshot contains eight pellets that are about .32 caliber. This is like shooting an intruder *eight times with a .32 caliber pistol in a single shot*. In an apartment setting or inside a house where drywall may separate you from neighbors or family members, consider something with less penetration such as number 4 buckshot.

Slugs and Sabot

A shotgun "slug" is a single projectile that is fired from a shot shell. Slugs are large, heavy chunks of lead that are an effective hunting tool for large or tough game such as deer, bear (small bear), wild boar, and Javalina. Slugs are favored in some states for hunting due to their short range. A hunter should not try to take game at over 150 yards with a slug. "Sabot" rounds are specially formed slugs that have a more aerodynamic profile (which improves downrange performance). In a sabot round, the projectile is encased in a "shell" that keeps the round oriented correctly in the barrel. Once the round exits the barrel, the sabot's fall away.

Slugs and sabot rounds may be fired from most shotguns; however, if the shotgun is has a removable choke tube, you want to use a "cylinder" choke tube. "Cylinder" choke tubes impart no constriction on the shot column (slug or sabot) as it leaves the barrel. Some manufacturers offer special slug barrels for their shotguns (either sold with the shotgun or as an aftermarket changeable barrel). These barrels are typically rifled to impart spin, and thus greater accuracy, for the slug or sabot.

Slugs and sabots for personal defense? While the idea of punching a single huge hole is attractive and would certainly "get the job done" in a defensive situation, the recoil of slugs and sabot are generally pretty severe. Overpenetration of wallboard is also a chief concern. So unless you're being attacked by a bear, it might be better to opt for buckshot. When I camp in country where bear or mountain lions might be present, I keep my twelve-gauge Remington 870 close by, loaded alternately with buckshot and slugs.

A Dram Here and a Dram There

When choosing your shotgun shells, you'll be faced with a lot of numbers and choices. So far, we've covered shot size and the length of the shell. The other critical number is the "Dram equivalent" of the shell. The first shotgun shells were loaded with black powder. Black powder was measured in drams (where modern smokeless powder is measured in grains). When smokeless powder came into use, people who loaded their own shells needed a way to equate the velocity of the smokeless round to what they were used to loading with black powder. They picked a "reference" charge of three drams of black powder with 1 1/8 oz. of shot. All smokeless loads are referenced against this benchmark. Basically, what this means to the consumer buying shotgun shells is that the higher the number, the more force/recoil that load will have. For sporting applications, stick to loads well below three. For waterfowl, turkey, and other big game hunting, go as high as you can comfortably shoot (that is appropriate for your shotgun).

CHAPTER

6

So I've Got a Gun, What Do I Do with It?

You've just gotten home from the gun store or gun show with your brand-new gun. Now comes the fun part. Enjoying your new purchase. Without a doubt, the *very first thing you should do is to read the manual* that comes with your new gun. The manual answer many questions like "What ammunition can I use," "How does the safety work," "How do I disassemble the firearm," and if you are lucky, "How do I *reassemble* the firearm." If you are buying a used firearm, it may not have the original, factory manual. A quick search of the Internet can usually turn one up. Ruger and SIG Sauer are very good about having product manuals available in .pdf file format, but other sites have manuals as well. Failing that, call the manufacturer. For liability reasons, they will be more than happy to send you a replacement manual.

It is important to know how to disassemble your firearm in order to clean and lubricate it adequately and to be able to fix any malfunctions that may occur.

Shortly after you arrive home with your gun, you should clean it to remove any additional factory packing lubrication left on the gun (most gun stores will do this before placing the gun out for sale; however, if you're buying a military surplus rifle, be prepared to spend a couple of hours with a bottle of paint thinner, removing the Cosmoline from the firearm).

The rest of this chapter covers the "care and feeding" of your new firearm.

Securing Your Gun

All gun owners have the responsibility to keep their guns out of unauthorized hands. In America, many states have laws on the books that require guns to be secured in a house with children. No one wants to be the lead story on the 11:00 PM news because their child found their "nightstand" gun and shot someone else's child. This chapter will show you how to prevent tragedy by useful ways to secure your firearms against accidents and theft.

Storing Guns in Cases or Holsters

Almost anyone who buys a gun and intends to carry it outside the home will purchase a case or holster to protect the finish from scratches or the effects of weather in transit. The natural tendency would be to keep the firearm in its protective case/holster once you return home. This logic accounts for a ruined finish on many a gun.

Most gun cases use a polystyrene or closed cell foam to protect the gun from scratches and impacts. It's inexpensive and very effective. *But* it is also a very effective moisture barrier. Meaning that it keeps moisture against the finish of your gun. This leads to surface rust which can ruin the external finish of the gun and lead to deterioration of the firearm's bore through a process known as "pitting" where rust actually eats a hole in the inside of the barrel. Stainless steel guns have a much greater resistance to rust than "blue steel" guns. In fact, the "bluing" process uses salts at high heat to form a protective, rustlike patina on the gun's parts.

The three most common materials for holsters are leather, ballistic nylon cloth/foam blends, and injection (or thermal) molded plastics. Storing a handgun in a leather or ballistic nylon holster can have the same effect as storing it in a case. Moisture and salts (from perspiration) can attack your gun's finish. Injection or thermally molded plastic holsters are much better but are not preferred by some more traditional shooters.

Your guns should be stored in a dry area where air can circulate around them.

Gun Safes

Gun safes run the gamut from small touch pad steel affairs to modified rooms in houses. Choosing the right safe (or safes) is a matter of preference, and budget. In this section, we'll look at gun safes from the least secure to the most secure and give some idea on price and features to look for.

WOOD GUN CABINETS

Beware buying nice gun cases to secure your firearms. While they make displaying firearms easy, a glass window doesn't do much to keep your guns secure. These are best suited for nonfiring heirlooms or in locations with low crime rates and no children. Anything made of wood and glass can be broken, usually with simple tools. As a result, wood gun cabinets rank lowest on the protection scale.

STEEL GUN CABINETS (LOW-END SAFES)

At the low end, several companies make gun safes that are constructed out of stamped steel and welded together. These are terrific "starter" safes for the new gun collector. They are relatively secure (taking barrel-type keys to open and usually having multiple locking lugs). Inside, these safes often have closed-cell foam lining to protect the guns' finish. Most feature predrilled holes to permit the owner to bolt the safe to a stud in their house. This is recommended for smaller safes where the entire unit may be "trucked out" of their home in a robbery. A popular model is made by the Stack-On company. Stack-On makes several models of safe from a small cabinet for hand guns to a double door model that holds about twelve long guns. Each are made of eight-gauge steel and feature pry-resistant doors. Many models may be attached to others (hence the name "stack on"). Remington also markets similar gun cabinets. An eight-gun model weighs in at about seventy pounds, so the risk that they'll go through your floor is minimal. These safes offer

Morton boot oak gun cabinet

Stack-on gun cabinet

zero fire protection and limited protection from a determined thief. They excel at what my daddy called "keeping the honest people out."

GUN SAFES

Most people consider a Cam locking system to be the basic component of a safe. A quick search of the Internet for "gun safes" will turn up thousands of hits. Look to Fort Knox, Century, and Browning for some of the best, but don't overlook other makers. The advantage of a gun safe is it's weight and (usually) fire protection. Most safes that are over twelve guns in size are assembled in your home. These safes weigh in at six hundred pounds or more, so make sure you don't want to move it after it's setup.

Prices are based on the features of the safe. On the low end, a stack-on safe with a simple combination lock and no fire resistance might only be a couple of hundred dollars, while a safe that offers three hours of fire protection and a digital keypad would run several thousand. These safes are typically sold by

- their capacity (number of guns stored),
- number of locking rods/cams,
- steel thickness,
- fire protection (so many minutes at a given temperature),
- locking mechanism (combination lock, vs. digital keypad, vs. key).

Due to their size and weight, many people will choose an out-of-the-way location for the safe (in a basement or utility room) where it might not be readily accessed in an emergency (like a home invasion or other break-in). As a result, you may need a second gun safe or secured gun in a bedroom.

KEEPING GUNS CLOSE AT HAND
While a large, heavy gun safe is the best way to secure your guns, they aren't necessarily the best home décor. As a result, trying to convince your wife that you need to set a refrigerator-sized gun safe in the bedroom can be a tough sell. If your goal is to have a gun safe at hand for personal defense, you'll need another strategy.

YOUR BASIC "BIG BOX" FIRE SAFE
A strategy that works well is to buy a basic "fire safe" from your local "big box" hardware or office supply store (Lowes, Home Depot, Office Depot, Staples, etc.). These safes are usually about 2' x 2' x 2' and secure your firearms, important papers, and other valuable items. Most also include mounting hardware to mount to a floor or vanity. These safes come with a variety of locking mechanisms; however, one with a lighted touch pad is

A collection of Ft. Knox gun safes

the best for personal defense as they are quick to access and don't require any keys.

TACTILE SAFES

Tactile gun safes are meant to be mounted in or on a nightstand. They feature a touch keypad that can be manipulated in total darkness and provide access to a firearm. Many are thin enough to mount inside a drawer while some must be set on top of a nightstand or dresser. Many of these safes can also be mounted in vehicles, making them a unique way to secure your handgun should you carry it outside your home. Examples of these

Sentry A3860 Model Fire Safe

safes include the HanDGUN Box © by R&D Enterprises, or the GunVault (www.gunvault.com). Each of these units are priced around $200.

TRIGGER LOCKS

Most guns sold today come with a gun lock or trigger lock. There are two main types, a trigger lock and an action lock. A trigger lock secures the gun by placing a locking mechanism on either side of the gun and connecting it through the trigger. Once secured, no one can manipulate the trigger without first removing the lock. Trigger locks come in both keyed and combination styles. The second most common lock is the action lock. These locks typically have a cable that feeds through the action of the gun and locks into a laminated lock body. These locks are a terrific way to secure

GunVault GV 2000 Multi

your gun against unauthorized access but require a key to be close at hand for an emergency. Naturally, they don't carry well.

INTERNAL GUN LOCKS

Many gun makers provide an "internal locking" mechanism on their firearms. These mechanisms lock the action so that the gun can not be fired unless the shooter unlocks the action. Smith & Wesson, Taurus, and Ruger

Trigger lock and action lock

all make handguns with a locking mechanism, but interest in this as a form of security is waning.

DEHUMIDIFIERS AND DESICCANTS

Most safes are predrilled to feed an electrical connection through for a dehumidifier or light. Adding a small, inexpensive heating coil such as a Goldenrod can protect your investment in firearms against rust and corrosion. Another option is to buy a suitable amount of a desiccant such as silica gel (motto: Do Not Eat) to your safe. These can be purchased online or in gun stores.

Cleaning Your Gun

As stated earlier, when you *do* buy your first gun, the most important "first step" is to thoroughly read and understand the manual. Also in the manual will be disassembly and (hopefully) reassembly instructions (yes, I've

Goldenrod Dehumidifier

taken a gun to a gunsmith, in parts, because I didn't know how to put it back together). Your manual should also include directions on how much disassembly is necessary for "routine" cleaning.

Firing your gun makes it dirty. A great deal of burnt and unburnt powder residue are deposited not only in the bore but in the action as well. As the bullet exits the barrel, it will deposit small amounts of copper or lead (depending on the type of bullet) in the barrel's rifling. If left unchecked, these deposits will have an adverse effect on the accuracy of the firearm and can become downright dangerous if not cleaned. Finally, a gun that "rides around in a purse" or even in a holster that is tucked into a waistband of trousers will attract all kinds of moisture, lint, dust, and salts (from perspiration). These can attack the finish of your firearm and can induce jams and stoppages. So even if you don't shoot your gun, you should still plan on cleaning it every four to six months (more if it makes you happy).

What Do I need to Clean a Gun?

A wise man once said that *"fishing lures were made to catch fishermen."* The corollary for the gun world is that *"gun-cleaning products were made to clean out the wallets of gun owners."* There are an amazing array of products out there all claiming to be the quickest, best, most through cleaners on the market. To decide what works best for you, start slow and work up to the "fancier" cleaners.

Most gun and sporting goods stores/departments have a "basic" gun cleaning kit. If you're new to guns, buy one. They are a good place to start. Your gun cleaning kit will contain a rod and rod accessories, a bottle of bore solvent, gun oil, and cloth patches. You'll also need to buy a "bore brush" that is the size of your firearm's bore. Other materials that will come in handy include an old toothbrush (or a new one, but dedicate it to gun cleaning), an old T-shirt (described as a "lint-free cloth" in most literature) a surface that can get oily and dirty, a small flashlight, several dental picks, cotton swabs, and needle-nose pliers.

First marketed in 1903, Hoppe's 9 is one of the best known gun cleaners in the world. Found in most stores it is the "old reliable" of gun cleaners. The liquid works by dissolving caked on powder and loosening lead and copper deposits in the barrel. This can then be removed by running patches (soaked in the solution) down the barrel and drawing them back and forth until a patch goes the full length of the bore without dramatically changing the color of the patch. Since Hoppe's degreases the barrel, a patch of oil should be run down the bore to protect it from rusting.

After using a solvent, a generous amount of gun oil (high-grade machine oil will work in a pinch). Dedicated gun oils such as those from Hoppe's and Remington are excellent lubricants for your firearm.

Ballistol is another popular gun-cleaning product. It was developed in Germany in the late 1800s as a single product that could clean and lubricate metal parts as well as preserve wood and leather. Ballistol works equally well on black powder as it does on smokeless powder. It can be a little hard to find unless you're looking in better gun stores or ordering online.

Hoppe's 9 Powder Solvent

Dunk-it baths are an interesting alternative to gun cleaning. These tubs come in various sizes and compositions (those that will work on Polymer frame guns like Glocks) and those that work on all-steel guns only. These tubs contain a chemical bath. First, the handgun's grips are removed. Then the whole gun is submerged in the liquid. After a predefined period of soaking, the gun is then removed and the excess liquid permitted to drain back into the tub.

Tetra Gun Grease – Grease is used to promote parts sliding across one another. This is useful where an oil-based lubricant might not be persistent enough to stand up to a lot of shooting.

WD-40 – is a wonderful product. It lubricates and cleans well. *However,* WD-40 is water based. As such, it can actually promote rust and corrosion on your gun and should be avoided unless it's followed up with another product such as Rem Oil.

You didn't mention my father's/uncle's/grandfather's/neighbor-down-the-road's gun cleaner. Well, you'd be right. As stated when this chapter started, there are a myriad of gun cleaners out there, most which work really well, but most do about the same thing . . . remove carbon fouling, lead, and copper buildup from your firearms. Go crazy, experiment. Just make sure you follow the instructions and avoid smoking while you clean.

How Do I Clean My Gun?

STEP 1 – Make sure your gun is unloaded! Most instructors will tell you that no one has accidentally been shot with a loaded gun. It was always the gun that somebody was darn sure *was unloaded* that somehow manages to shoot someone. If you follow the rules of gun etiquette, you'll check to make sure it's empty first, prior to disassembly to clean, *always*.

STEP 2 – Start with a clean area with enough room for your cleaning tools and the disassembled firearm. Make sure that you have adequate light to see *that spring* that *will magically* jump across the room if you aren't paying close enough attention. Also make sure you allow enough time to do the job properly. If you hurry, you might forget to reassemble the firearm correctly, which could lead to disaster.

STEP 3 – Disassemble your firearm per manufacturer's instructions. For most cleaning, this is minimal. For revolvers, it usually means just disassembling the crane to remove the cylinder. For semiautomatic pistols, it usually entails removing the slide from the frame and the barrel and recoil spring/guide from the slide. Rifles and shotguns vary but are usually simpler still to disassemble to a point necessary for routine cleaning.

STEP 4 – Wipe all pieces down with clean, dry cloth. This will remove 90 percent of the dirt and will keep your work site cleaner.

STEP 5 - Brush out the bore with the wire brush to remove the majority of the fouling. If you are cleaning a revolver, brush out each chamber in the cylinder too.

STEP 6 – Coat a gun-cleaning patch in bore solvent and run it through the bore using a "jag" accessory tip. Repeat this step until the gun patch comes out the same color as it went in (four to five will usually do it). Again, if you are cleaning a revolver, repeat this process on each chamber.

STEP 7 – Using a soft bristle brush dipped in solvent, brush off any surface that might have become fouled. This includes the outside (front and

1911 semiautomatic pistol field stripped for cleaning

rear) of a revolver's cylinder, the inside of the slide on a semiautomatic, the chamber of a lever-action rifle or shotgun, the outside of the barrel, etc.

STEP 8 – Wipe off all excess powder solvent with a soft, dry cloth.

STEP 9 – Run a patch that is *lightly* lubricated with oil down the bore (and each chamber of a revolver).

STEP 10 – Apply lubricant to the firearm. My rule of thumb is that if it is a part that moves it gets oiled. If it's a part that slides against another part, it gets grease, but a single lubricant will work for most people.

STEP 11 – Reassemble the firearm per manufacturer's instructions and wipe off excess oil. Store your gun in a safe, dry environment.

What to Do If Something Breaks?

A firearm is a machine. As a machine, if it is used enough, something will wear out or break. If this happens, you face the same choice as you do with your vehicle: take it to a repair facility or fix it yourself.

Warranty Work

Most firearms come with a warranty just like an automobile. Most firearm warranties are much better too. Often they will cover the firearm for the owner's lifetime, but some have important exceptions. For instance, if you have installed aftermarket parts into a Ruger revolver, and return the handgun for service, Ruger will replace your aftermarket parts with the latest factory fresh parts (they will typically return your aftermarket parts as well). Working on some guns (or having a gunsmith attempt to repair them first) can actually void the warranty on certain guns. If in doubt, consult your firearms owner's manual before you try to make any repairs.

In many cases, all you have to do is call the customer service number for the manufacturer and they will cover the gun's shipment both to and from the factory. Once the firearm has been received from the factory, a service technician will review the firearm and contact you to advise you of what they found. After the gun has been repaired, it will be shipped back to your door.

Gunsmiths

Returning a firearm to the manufacturer is not the only option for repairs, upgrades, and modifications. The local gunsmith is usually a faster alternative. Gunsmiths are machinists that specialize in firearms. While many trade schools offer degree programs in "gunsmithing," there is not a licensing requirement for someone to go into the "gunsmithing business," so, buyer, beware. The best gunsmiths are found by word of mouth. Ask around at the range or your local gun store. Many stores have a gunsmith who is resident in the store and can do your work there; some contract gunsmith work outside or will make referrals. If you are finding a gunsmith through a telephone directory, ask for references of people whose guns have been worked on by the smith.

But repairs are only a small fraction of what a gunsmith can do for you and your gun. A gunsmith can make modifications or install aftermarket parts that make your firearm perform at a higher level than an "out of the box" firearm. Consider the difference between a car that comes off the production line versus one that's been tuned for racing by a top NASCAR technician. You start to get an idea of what a good gunsmith can do for you. One of the most common tasks for a gunsmith (outside of repair) is to do an "action job" on a firearm. To perform an action job, the gunsmith carefully disassembles and inspects all the parts that bear against each other. These are carefully polished to reduce friction. Springs are usually adjusted, lightened, or replaced to make the action easier to operate. Other work may include "porting" the barrel to vent escaping gases up. This has the effect of reducing felt recoil. On long guns (rifles and shotguns), it is common to have the "length of pull"[10] adjusted to fit the shooter and a recoil pad fit to the gun. Ultimately, a gun will have a part that wears out that can't be replaced by ordinary means. Most people don't have the facilities to change out a barrel. This usually requires the special tools that a well-stocked gunsmith will have at hand.

Gunsmith services don't stop there. A true master can construct a gun that is built to your dimensions. Custom-fit rifles and shotguns don't come cheap but are considered worth the price by those who can afford them.

So when do you decide to go to a gunsmith rather than send a gun back? I normally go to the gunsmith first. It could be a minor adjustment that would only take a moment versus a two-week to several-month wait while a large manufacturer repairs your gun (depends largely on backlog). If the repair is inexpensive enough and doesn't void any warranties, then I'll go with the gunsmith.

Learn to Shoot – Take Lessons

OK, another "golf metaphor." A beginner shooter taking shooting lessons is like a beginning golfer taking golfing instruction. It's just a good idea to have someone who really knows what they are doing *and more important,*

---

10 Length of pull is the distance from the butt end of the stock to the front of the trigger.

how to teach that to others, show you the ropes. This will keep you from developing bad habits and will put you on the right path toward developing the proper stance, sight picture, and grip (sounds more and more like golf doesn't it?).

Can't my husband/father/best friend Earl just take me out and teach me?

Perhaps, but I've been married a *long* time and intend to stay married. One of the secrets that I've learned is that it's best if I don't try to "teach" my spouse anything; however, we do *great* learning together. Most people, even life-long shooters, don't necessarily shoot correctly. Believe me, taking a course, even for an advanced shooter, is beneficial.

I've shot for years, why should I get lessons now?

When I first started shooting Cowboy Action Shooting, I would normally finish in the "lower half of the pack." After about two years, I took a couple of courses from a renowned instructor Joe West. Now I finish in the top half, and usually in the top 30 percent

How do I find a course?

Most gun ranges and better gun shops will be able to recommend a shooting instructor. It is best to find one who is certified by the National Rifle Association (NRA). Here in Georgia, I personally can recommend Walt Sippel (770-535-0029 or learntoshoot@hotmail.com) or Joe West (404-261-4869, or jjjwest@mindspring.com).

The best instruction is a "one-on-one" course that can be tailored to your needs and experience level. Here is a sample agenda from Walt's brochure:

1. Safety
2. Basic Firearm Identification
3. Ammunition Identification
4. Stance
5. Grip
6. Sight Picture
7. Trigger Control
8. Follow Through
9. Cleaning and Storage

Carrying Your Handgun

Most handgun owners have a drawer full of holsters. Some will even have holsters for guns that they no longer own! I've been known to buy a holster that was on good sale simply because I was planning on buying a gun that might fit it down the road. One explanation of this phenomenon is *"that holsters breed in dark places."* I've tried to use this one with my wife, but so far she's not buying it. She calls me the "Imelda Marcos" of holsters.

So why do you need a holster? Holsters are handy little items. If you are going to the range, a holster can protect the finish of your gun as it travels to and from the range. At the range, it gives you a convenient place to hold your gun while setting or retrieving targets. Naturally, if you plan on carrying a gun for personal defense or hunting, a holster is a very useful item to have. Likewise, most sports that involve a handgun (like IPSC, PPC, IDPA, Cowboy Action Shooting) require you to have one (or sometimes two) holsters.

IMPORTANT: Before carrying your gun in public, familiarize yourself with the state and local rules for your area. Most states (forty-three at this writing) offer a concealed carry license (CCL) to their citizens. *Failure to carry your gun legally can carry stiff penalties and even jail time.*

Holster Basics

All holsters have elements in common. As you evaluate holsters, these are aspects that you'll need to consider:

The first element is "retention." Retention is the method by which the holster keeps the handgun from falling out when the shooter does not actively draw the weapon. The most common form of retention is a strap that goes over the "mouth" of the holster, thus trapping the handgun inside. These work very well, but if you are carrying a gun for personal protection, it can hinder your draw in an emergency. As a result, some other forms of retention should be considered. A second form of retention is the "thumb break." A thumb break is a modification of the retention strap, but the snap is situated high on the strap where the owner's thumb can catch it and open it as part of the draw. This offers positive retention and quick access to the firearm. Still another form of retention is the "retention screw." Retention screws are built into the holster themselves and permit the user to "pinch" the holster's sides together tighter. This holds the gun firmer in the holster.

Another important aspect of holster design is "cant." Cant is the angle that the holster/handgun sits at relative to the ground. A holster that is canted is easier to draw from a concealed position. Typical cant values are from five to fifteen degrees.

Holster Materials

Early holsters were made of leather. In the early days of holsters, leather was used primarily because it was inexpensive, plentiful, and there were

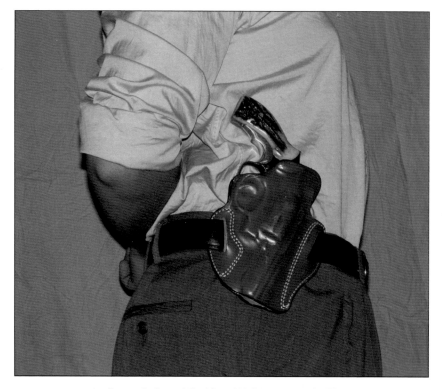

Desantis Speed Scabbard Holster canted 15°

plenty of people to do the work. Most early leather holsters were made by people who made saddles and harness gear for horses, mule, and oxen teams. Leather is still a popular holster material. It retains its shape, very comfortable to wear, and looks very "classy."

Leather holsters are typically molded to the gun that they are intended to carry. This process is typically called "wet molding." In this process, the leather is immersed in water almost to the point of saturation. A mold of the gun is then placed into the holster, and a small tool is used to push the leather into place around the "bumps and bulges" of the particular firearm. This process is called "boning." Once molded, the holster itself offers very good retention qualities. Once "broken in," a leather holster is very comfortable to wear. This is especially true if the holster is to be worn inside the pants where the holster will come into contact with the wearer's skin or undergarments.

When looking at leather holsters, one of the first items you'll have to decide on is to buy a lined or unlined holster. "Lining" is the process of sewing one piece of leather to another so that it has a finished surface on both the outside and the inside (facing the gun). Lined holsters fetch a premium over their unlined brethren due to the extra work and materials required to make these holsters. The advantage is that these holsters keep their shape better than unlined holsters and offer more protection for the finish of your handgun. Leather holsters in general make it easy to reholster your firearm without having to hold the holster open with the other hand. The downside of a lined holster is that it tends to be bulkier than an unlined holster and tends to "grab" the gun on drawing.

Leather does have its drawbacks. Like any natural material, leather tends to hold moisture. If your leather holster gets wet, you need to clean and carefully dry it to prevent mold and mildew buildup. Dry leather too quickly and it will crack. Remember, firearms should not be stored for long periods in leather holsters. Since the leather holds moisture in, it can lead to rust and corrosion in your firearm.

Another popular material for holsters is "ballistic nylon." Ballistic nylon holsters start as cloth that is composed of woven strips of nylon, a synthetic fiber. The cloth is frequently bound to a foam rubber backing for extra cushioning, and the edges are bound to prevent fraying. The material is then sewn to fit the outline of the holster. Nylon holsters are terrific for very humid climates because the holster can be periodically washed and dried without hurting the holster. The drawback to nylon holsters is that they tend to close after the gun has been drawn, so it is difficult to re-holster your firearm with one hand. Also, if the holster is worn inside the waistband, a nylon holster won't cushion the handgun as much as a leather holster will, making them less comfortable to wear for extended periods.

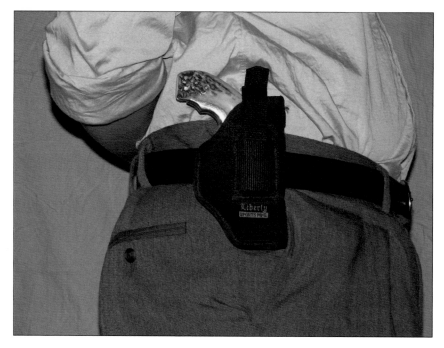

Nylon holster

"Kydex" is a revolutionary thermoplastic that is available in sheets or can be injection molded. It is lightweight, durable, impervious to moisture and body salts, normal temperatures ranges, chemical gun cleaners and lubricants. This material is cut and formed to a mold of the firearm using heat. Just like a leather holster, these holsters are typically boned to fit the firearm. This offers excellent retention qualities, but offers a smooth draw for the user. Kydex holsters have become very popular with competition shooters in the IDPA, IPSC/USPPC, and NRA Action Pistol. Most holster manufacturers offer some products produced in Kydex.

Kydex holsters differ from other plastic injection molded holsters made from different grades of plastic (styrene) in its superior shape retention and strength. Plastic injection molded holsters such as those from Fobus generally have to be thicker to accomplish the same retention characteristics as Kydex, but offer a great value for the money.

Thermoplastic Kydex holster with Smith and Wesson 625 Revolver

"Web Cloth" Cotton holsters have been made and issued to military units at different points in history. Occasionally one will turn up in a "miscellaneous bin" or on eBay. These holsters are as serviceable as any but don't typically keep their shape and hold moisture against the gun, so they aren't the best choice for a holster.

Types of Holsters

Most holsters are described by their material (leather, Kydex, etc), and how they are worn by the wearer. This section list the types of holsters typically found in the market.

OWB

The most popular type of holsters are those worn outside the waistband of the trousers. These holsters are typically abbreviated as "OWB holsters." An OWB holster usually has one or more loops that attach to a belt on the user's waist. The advantages of an OWB holster are easy accessibility and superior comfort. The drawback to an OWB is that they tend to be bulky and hard to conceal.

The most common form of OWB are those that have a single loop that attach to the wearer's belt on their dominate or "strong side." Strong side OWB holsters can hang straight down or be canted for easier draw.

Tooled leather strong side holster with retaining strap

Another popular way to carry a handgun is to wear the gun on the opposite side (or "weak side") with the gun's butt facing forward. The handgun is drawn by reaching across the body and grabbing the grip of the gun. This is known as "cross draw." Cross draw holsters are popular with people who hunt and those who spend a lot of time in the driver's seat of a car (like a police detective). Hunters often prefer a cross draw because they carry their rifle on a sling over their dominate shoulder. If they are wearing an OWB on the same side, the two guns will tend to collide with each other, causing damage to the finish of the rifle and the handgun. People who spend a great deal of time driving may opt for a cross draw because it's easier to draw from a seated position than a strong-side holster.

A holster that is made of two layers of material sewn together on either side of the handgun is referred to as a "pancake holster." Pancake holsters offer greater concealment than a typical OWB holster. The double belt slots tend to pull the holster into the body and tight, so the pancake holster offers superior retention. Pancake holsters may have a thumb break or be open top (as pictured below).

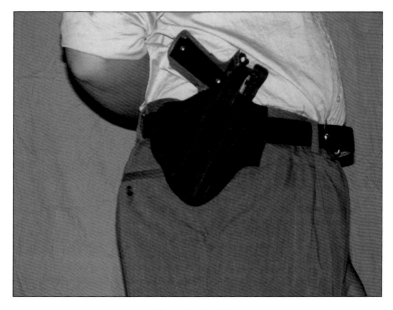

Pancake holster

Holsters that are made to be worn in the middle of ones back are referred to as "small of the back" holsters or SOB. These holsters are easy to hide under an untucked shirt, vest, or sport coat but aren't very comfortable if you're seated for a long period of time.

PADDLE HOLSTERS

Another popular class of holster is the paddle holster. Unlike traditional OWB holsters, the "paddle holster" has an attachment that slides into the waistband of the wearer's trousers. This permits the wearer to tuck the holster into their pants without having to thread unbuckle and unthread a belt through their pants. Also, if the gun is light enough, a paddle holster can support a gun without a belt at all (but this isn't usually recommended). Paddle holsters are very useful if the user usually wears a gun but must take it on and off frequently (like going in and out of buildings where guns can not be legally carried). The drawback to a paddle holster is that they are typically harder to conceal due to the fact that they stick out further from the body to accommodate the addition of the paddle.

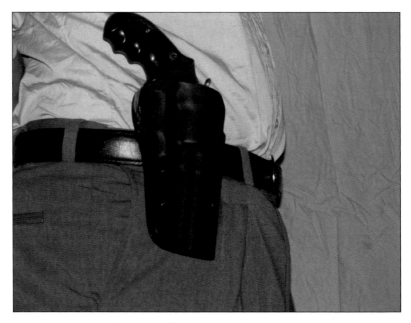

Kydex paddle holster - outside view

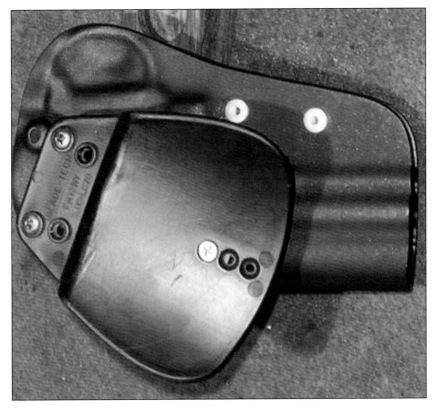

Blade-tech paddle holster - paddle detail

IWB

Perhaps the best way to conceal a firearm is in a "inside the waistband" holster or IWB for short. An IWB holster tucks the gun side the trousers at the waistband. Plastic, leather, or steel loops then attach to the belt over the top of the trousers. A recent development are hooks that attach to the holster deeper inside the pants. This permits a shirttail to be "tucked" between the holster and trousers, thus enhancing the concealability of the holster. The disadvantage of IWB holsters is that they take up a lot of space in your pants and are frequently uncomfortable. They can also be difficult to install and remove if you need to go into a building where you can not legally carry your gun (even with a CCL).

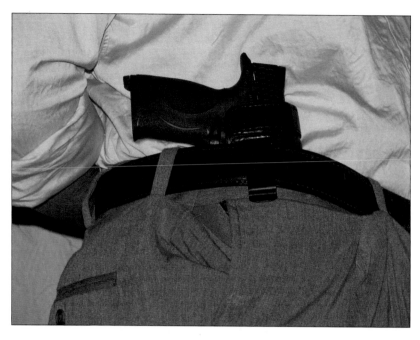

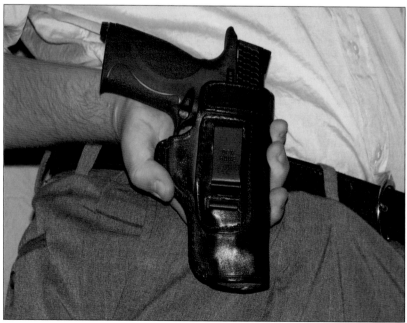

Don Hume M-715 holster with Smith and Wesson M&P

POCKET HOLSTER

Pocket holsters are meant to protect your handgun when placed in either a front or back pocket, although they are also useful for coats, jackets, and purses. Often a person won't want to "strap on leather" just to run down to the store or walk the dog. This is especially true in warm environments where concealing a gun can be very difficult in the summer. In these cases, a small gun can be easily slipped into a front shorts pocket. Having a "pocket holster" can be beneficial in a number of ways. For instance, a good pocket holster will hide the gun's outline in your pocket. This is especially useful when you sit down with the gun in your front pocket or have it in your rear pocket with tight-fitting pants. A pocket holster will keep lint from building up in the action of the gun (which can prevent normal feeding in small automatics). Pocket holsters permit one's gun to also be drawn without "snagging" on other objects in one's pockets. Finally, a pocket holster will protect the gun's finish from keys, change, and everything else that may be in one's pockets.

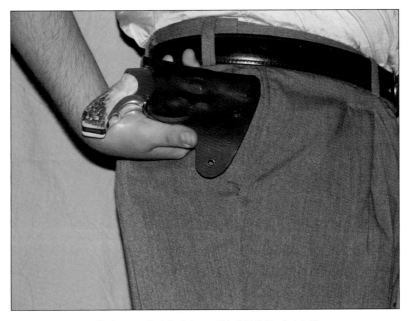

Kydex pocket holster with S&W Model 640

SHOULDER

Shoulder holsters conjure up images of James Bond, Dirty Harry, Sonny Crockett (*Miami Vice*), or other serious gun-toter. A "shoulder holster" is a holster that is worn under one's arm, with a harness that goes behind the back which the other arm is passed through. This permits the firearm to be suspended under the arm and either horizontally or vertically. Extra magazines can be worn on the opposite side of the holster to balance out the load. Shoulder holsters are not just for concealed carry. Many handgun hunters will use shoulder holsters to transfer the weight of their large handgun from their waist to their shoulders and to offer more protection for a scoped handgun (from brush and obstacles that might scratch or catch a scope if worn on the hip).

Shoulder holsters have several advantages over OWB or IWB holsters. Shoulder holsters are easily concealed under a jacket or coat. The firearm is easily accessible while the wearer is seated. A shoulder holster takes weight off the wearer's waist. This can be a benefit for soldiers who work in confined areas such as tanks and aircraft (see picture).

Galco Miami Classic

Shoulder holsters are not for everyone. A shoulder holster must be worn under a shirt or jacket *all the time* to stay concealed. This can be difficult in warm weather environments. The complexity of shoulder holsters also tend to make them expensive. Expect to pay over $150 for a good one such as the "Miami Classic" by Galco which was made famous by the TV show *Miami Vice*.

ANKLE HOLSTER

Ankle holsters are typically a holster of last resort for people who are already carrying a firearm. Most professionals who carry guns (law enforcement, personal protection, bounty hunters, etc.) carry more than one firearm. Undercover officers typically can't wear their duty leather or any other type of holster that may be observable by the suspects with which they are interacting. As the name implies, "ankle holsters" attach a gun to the wearer's ankle or calf, under a pants' leg. This keeps the firearm out of sight to all but the most detailed of searches. Another advantage of an ankle holster is that the user can usually reach the holster from a seated position (either in a car or by crossing a leg under a table). However, having an ankle holster can also be a drawback. First, unless a very small firearm is carried, the weight can be uncomfortable and can even throw off one's balance. They are not very comfortable and care must be taken to keep pants long enough to *always* cover the firearm. Also, drawing the weapon from a standing position is awkward and forces the owner off balance to retrieve the firearm. This is never a "good thing" in a gunfight.

YAQUI SLIDES

A "Yaqui slide" holster is designed to be worn on the belt (OWB fashion) yet be composed of the minimum of leather. Chuck Norris's character in *Walker Texas Ranger* used a Yaqui slide once he switched to a Taurus semiautomatic (about the second or third season). Most Yaqui holsters are molded to the shape of a single gun. Some, such as the excellent "sippel solution" (see photo below) can holster almost any pistol from the most diminutive semiautomatic to a large frame revolver, being more of a hybrid between an actual Yaqui slide and a pancake holster.

The same advantages and disadvantages for an OWB holster apply to a Yaqui slide. They tend to stick out more than an IWB and are be pretty obviously holsters even when the gun is removed.

The Sippel Solution holster

SPECIALTY/NOVELTY

Inevitably, there is always an "other" section. Anyone who has seen a "secret agent" movie has seen all the ways that you could possibly hide a gun. This section list some of the ones that the new gun owner will find in the marketplace.

Fanny Packs

The "fanny pack" is the ubiquitous symbol of a tourist. And why not. They are a handy way to carry a camera in reasonable security without bulging pockets. Several manufacturers offer "fanny pack holsters." The better units have the fanny pack that covers a holster. The fanny pack portion is sewn at the bottom and is then attached to the holster portion by Velcro. A quick tug on the corner of the fanny pack reveals the holster with the firearm ready to draw. Many are offered in both small and large sizes. Since fanny pack gun systems have been on the market almost as long as fanny packs, their value as a concealment system is questionable.

Purses / Organizers

Several holster/leather manufacturers have backpacks and purses that have concealed pockets for guns in them. Many of the purses have a over-sized strap so that they can be comfortably worn "over the shoulder" or "over the head and one shoulder" for extra security. The owner's hand can be slipped into the holster pocket from the rear of the purse and kept on the gun. If absolutely necessary, a revolver can be fired through the purse (but it's not recommended). Many of these purses have been on the market for several years. When I suggested on to my wife, her comment was that most were "butt ugly," but tastes vary.

Day Planners & Leather zippered organizers have also been pressed into service as a way to "carry a gun in plain sight." These units look just like their brethren but have a secret compartment for the holster. Depending on the size of the day planner, you can conceal a pretty-good-size gun and an extra magazine or two.

PagerPal / Thunderware

Another popular idea are holsters that are made into items intended to wear under clothes against the body. A good example of this is Thunder-ware. This is a holster system that is worn around the waist. The firearm lays flat against the lower thigh and can be drawn by slipping one's hand down the front of their pants. This method really doesn't work very well if you have some extra pounds as there tends to be a bulge in the way of the gun lying flat. The PagerPal is a special form of an IWB holster that completely conceals into the wearer's trousers. On the outside of the holster is an attachment point for a pager (a fake pager comes with the unit) or a cell phone. To draw the weapon, the owner simply pulls up on the pager/phone until the butt of the handgun is visible and then draws the gun. Again, this solution doesn't work well for heavyset people such as myself.

PagerPal holster

Shooting Ranges

Once one has bought a gun, the question becomes "Where can I fire it?" Unfortunately, the answer is becoming harder and harder to find. Hours of fun can be had in informal shooting on private land, but as civilization encroaches on the countryside, restrictions on gunfire usually follows. So if you don't have access to ten or so acres, where do you go? First, let your fingers do the walking and check the local phonebook or the Internet. Depending on where you live, you'll find a wealth of places to shoot including indoor gun ranges, outdoor gun ranges (public and private), gun clubs, and even public ranges paid for with your tax dollars.

Indoor

Indoor ranges are the best bet for people who live in larger metropolitan areas. The noise of firing can be sufficiently baffled and the safety of neighboring areas ensured. Most often, an indoor range will be limited to handguns, rifles that shoot pistol-caliber rounds, or rimfire rifles. High-power rifles are difficult to corral, so many ranges don't even try.

Here's what to expect when you go to an indoor range. First you'll have to fill out a waiver and application to shoot. Most ranges will also keep your driver's license or military ID card while you shoot. Some ranges will also require that you buy your ammunition from them. While this practice is generally not well thought of, you must respect the owner's investment and liability. Some shooters will "roll their own" rounds, and who knows how powerful they might be. Other ranges might want you to use their ammunition if you are renting their guns. Generally, most ranges will let you use your own cartridges in your guns. You'll typically have to purchase one or more paper targets from the range. Eye and ear protection is required and is also available for rent (should you not have your own and everyone should). You then are ready to shoot.

You'll most likely be assigned a shooting position or booth. Inside your booth, you'll find controls for the target holder. You clip your target to the holder and advance it to the desired distance. Often, the distance is marked on the floor. Other times, common distances are indicated by lights that shine down from the ceiling. These distances are typically seven yards, fifteen yards, twenty-five yards, and fifty yards (range permitting). At this point, you are ready to load and discharge your firearm. You'll be able to bring your target back at anytime you wish. Be prepared. Indoor ranges can be *very* loud, even with hearing protection. Just remember the safe gun handling we discussed in the section on "gun etiquette" and the 10 Commandments of Gun Safety.

When you are finished, you should secure your firearm(s), retrieve your target, remove any brass that's in the immediate area, and exit the booth to check out and get your identification back.

Many indoor ranges offer memberships. Others charge by the half hour or hour. Deciding which way to go depends on how much shooting you intend to do. Many ranges also have leagues (much like a bowling league) that offer friendly competition.

Oakwood Sportsman's Lodge Indoor Shooting Facility, Oakwood, Georgia

Outdoor

I've always enjoyed shooting outside more than inside. Most outdoor shooting ranges are affiliated with a gun store of some kind. Most do not rent firearms, but there is always an exception. The main difference between the procedure for shooting at an outdoor facility as opposed to an indoor facility is that periodically, fire is stopped for people to place their targets on the range. This is either called by a range officer who oversees the shooting or by a general agreement by all the shooters on the line. When the line is called "safe," you should immediately stop firing, remove all rounds from your guns, open the actions, and step back from the firing line. Once everyone has stepped back from the line, the range will be declared safe, and you'll be instructed to go downrange to set, inspect, or retrieve your target. Also when shooting on an outside range, it is usually up to the shooter to police their own used brass. As with indoor ranges, many outdoor ranges offer memberships and host competitions.

Gun Clubs

Gun clubs are private organizations that exist to provide their members a place to shoot and (usually) organized events/competitions to shoot in. Gun clubs are similar to golf courses. Some permit nonmembers to come shoot and some do not. Many clubs don't have full-time employees. Best to call the club, leave a message if nobody answers. Somebody should get back in touch with you to let you know the status of membership or if nonmembers are permitted to shoot.

Public Ranges

Some gun ranges are operated by municipal authorities or the State Department of Natural Resources. These ranges are often found on Wildlife Management Areas. For instance, Georgia has fifteen ranges on WMA land. Most of these ranges are not staffed. Shooters are expected to follow range rules like responsible adults who are permitted to own guns.

Competition

Competition! Are you as intimidated as I was? Even after I had been shooting for several years, I never thought that I'd try to shoot against anyone else. That was until I attended my first Cowboy Action Shooting match. I expected a lot of "surly old men" who were dour and serious about their guns. I found a mix of men, women, and children have "the most fun you can have with your clothes on." After that positive experience, I jumped in with both feet. Since starting to shoot competitively, I've branched out and

100 Yard General Purpose Range at Cherokee Gun Club

tried other sports like IHMSA, trap, sporting clays, skeet, and plan to try IPSC and IDPA.

Joining a competitive shooting sport reinforces good shooting habits. It also gives you a *"reason"* to go out shooting other than simply punching holes in paper. Going to matches also puts you in touch with other people who can teach you how to shoot better and instruct you in buying gear based on "real world" experiences and not on an advertisement in a magazine. This is not even to mention the positive aspects of being outside with friends getting some exercise and fellowshipping.

When I started shooting, I bought guns to justify my "hunting habit." But after five years of hunting, I realized that I still had some of the same hunting bullets I started hunting with (of course, I was never a very good hunter). I can go to a Cowboy Action match and shoot sixty rifle bullets, sixty pistol bullets, and a box of shotgun shells in a few hours. The object is to do something you'll enjoy and give you something else to do with your firearm. So even if competitive shooting isn't for you, take a look at a very few of the types of shooting you can do with other people. Finally, this chapter just scratches the surface of competitive shooting. There are many more types of shooting competitions available.

Cowboy Action Shooting

One of the most popular nonshotgun sports is Cowboy Action Shooting, or CAS. Cowboy Action Shooting was started by a group of people who enjoyed shooting the IPSC style of "running and gunning" but wanted to use their old single-action pistols, lever-action rifles, double-barrel, and pump shotguns. The governing body of the sport is the Single-action Shooting Society, or SASS. Since its inception in the early' 80s, the core group of founders (nicknamed "the Wild Bunch" after the 1969 Sam Peckinpah picture) have seen the ranks of registered shooters climb above seventy thousand. The sport is popular not only in the United States but is also shot in Canada, Great Britain, Norway, Finland, Switzerland, Germany, the Netherlands, the Czech Republic, Italy, Spain, New Zealand, and Australia.

Shooters compete with "pre-1900" style firearms that have been approved by SASS. All main match pistols must be single-actions. Rifles are predominately lever-action but a few pump-action rifles are permitted as well. Shotguns can be double barreled (with or without hammers), lever-action, or pump (with an external hammer). Shooters negotiate a course of fire (called a stage or scenario) with a group of other shooters (called a "posse"). Shooters shoot lead bullets only (no jacketed or hollow-point rounds) at steel targets. They are scored on the time it takes to navigate the course. Missed targets and failing to shoot targets in order (procedural penalties) add time to the score. While one shooter is shooting the stage, the other posse-members share the work details.

Joe West (alias "Joe West") shooting a replica Winchester 1866

A common misconception is that CAS is a "historical recreation" of the Old West that is similar to the people who participate in Civil War reenactments. CAS is really a fantasy sport based on the myths, legends, movies, and lore of the Old West. To reinforce this, all competitors must adopt and register a unique alias with SASS headquarters. This "alias" is how the shooter is known to the SASS community. In fact, after participating in this game for over six years, I have some people I consider *very* close friends who's "real name" is unknown to me. Rather I know them as "Stinky Jim," or "Hogleg Smith," or "Wicked Wanda." Often aliases are taken from historical figures or Western characters and actors. My own alias is Rolan Kraps, my son is Shootin' Kraps, and my wife is Bea Itchin'.

IPSC match being shot

To find out more about Cowboy Action Shooting and the Single-action Shooting Society, visit http://www.sassnet.com.

International Practical Shooting Confederation (IPSC) – United States Practical Shooting Association (USPSA)

Perhaps the "granddaddy" of all "action"-based shooting sports is IPSC. The sport is enjoyed worldwide in countries where civilian gun ownership is permitted. Founded in mid-1970s IPSC boasts over fifteen thousand current members in the United States alone, and their numbers are on the rise as more shooters discover the sport.

IPSC is primarily a "pistol sport." Participants navigate a course of fire shooting at paper targets and some steel "knockdown" targets. Paper targets are scored. When the targets are scored, hits in the center of the target count more than hits on the edge. After the targets have been scored, the holes are "pasted" over, and the next shooter runs through the course.

Virtually any serviceable pistol or revolver may be used for IPSC competition. Based on the handgun you use and other equipment and the power of your ammunition, the shooter competes in one of several "divisions." Contestants are further organized by their "classification scores." Classifications group shooters by their relative ability so that a brand new shooter doesn't have to go head to head against a "grandmaster" (the "Tiger Woods" classification of IPSC shooters). This makes it fun for the new shooter and the old pro alike.

Division	Characteristics
Limited Division	The limited division is recognized as the most popular division. Shooters typically shoot "wide-body" semiautomatic pistols that support high capacities (some shooters have up to thirty-round magazines). Shooters in Limited division may add minor external parts, but may not port or otherwise compensate their handguns, nor may they add optical sights.
Open Division	The Open Division is where the "race guns" live. These guns can have virtually any practical modification made to them. Compensated barrels, optical sights, beveled magazine wells, etc.
Revolver Division	The Revolver Division is open for "wheel-gun shooters." Capacities are limited to six rounds with no optical sights, porting, or recoil compensations. Shooters may change grips, enlarge the cylinder release, and make internal modifications and tuning.

Production Division	This is a new and rapidly growing division in IPSC. Shooters in the production division must use standard production guns. Only very limited modifications may be made to the gun (sights, internal action tuning, grip enhancements). Additionally, the shooter must use a holster that is intended for daily wear (as opposed to a "competition specific holster). Shooters are limited to ten rounds in their magazines.
Limited-10 Division	This division is intended for semiautomatic pistols that are limited to ten rounds in their magazines. Competitors can make modifications to their guns but may not add optical sights or port the barrels.

Another type of IPSC match is the "3-Gun Match." In a 3-Gun Match, the IPSC shooter uses their existing handgun, a semiautomatic rifle (such as an AR-15), and a shotgun (usually a pump or semiautomatic).

To find out more about IPSC and USPSA, check out their website at www.ipsc.org.

International Defensive Pistol Association (IDPA)

The International Defensive Pistol Association (IDPA) a shooting sport that evolved from IPSC and claims over eleven thousand members in nineteen countries. While the emphasis in IPSC is "running and gunning," the emphasis in IDPA is to shoot "realistic" shooting scenarios that would enhance the participants' ability to defend themselves with a gun (should it be necessary).

What this means to the shooter is that they must use a "stock" gun (minor modifications, as opposed to full-out race guns that can be found in some IPSC divisions), must use duty ammo (as opposed to the generally lighter loads that Cowboy Action Shooters use), and must use holsters that are practical for everyday carry.

This is a very easy sport to get involved in because the "average" shooter can compete with items that they most likely already have: a pistol (revolver or semiautomatic), some extra magazines or speed loaders, and a holster. The handgun doesn't need expensive modifications to be competitive.

Per the IDPA website: "The firearms are grouped into five (5) divisions: 1) Custom Defensive Pistol (.45ACP semiautomatics only); 2) Enhanced Service Pistol (9 mm [9 x 19] or larger caliber semiautomatics); 3) Stock Service Pistol (9 mm [9 x 19] or larger caliber double-action, double-action only, or safe action semiautomatics); 4) Enhanced Service Revolver (.38 caliber or larger double-action revolvers); and 5) Stock Service Revolver (.38 caliber or larger double-action revolvers). See Appendix One – Equipment for delineations in the revolver divisions. Shooters are then classed by like-skill levels with progression from Novice (NV); to Marksman (MM); to Sharpshooter (SS); to Expert (EX); and, finally, to Master (MA)."

For more information, visit www.idpa.com.

Black Powder Cartridge Rifle (BPCR)

This unique sport harkens back to the first fully metallic cartridges (which were originally loaded with black powder). In this sport, competitors shoot these fine old cartridges loaded with real black powder or modern substitutes. The guns must be original or modern replicas of the cartridge rifles that existed in the 1870s to the introduction of smokeless powder. These include Sharps rifles, Trapdoor Springfield rifles, Remington Rolling Blocks, Winchester High Wall rifles, Ballard rifles, and many others. The use of sights is heavily regulated by the BPCR rules.

In this game, the shooter must engage steel targets at distances of up to five hundred meters! The targets vary in size to match known distances and consist of chickens, pigs, turkeys, and rams. Shooters must alter their position as they shoot. Typically, they will shoot a number of targets standing, another group sitting, another prone, and another standing without bracing the gun (off-hand).

For more information on Black Powder Cartridge Rifle competition, check out www.bpcr.net.

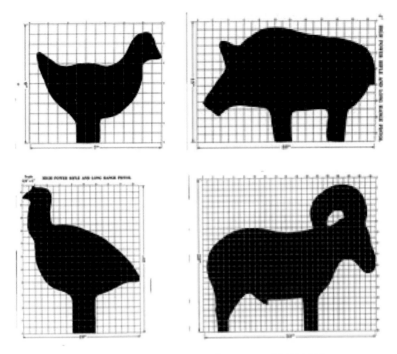

Sample target silhouettes **from** www.BPCR.NET

International Handgun Metallic Shooting (IHMSA)

One of the most challenging shooting sports is the International Hand-gun Metallic Silhouette Association or IHMSA. This sport was founded in 1976 and has a small but demented following. Shooters in IHMSA shoot at twenty-five, fifty, seventy-five, and a hundred yards at steel targets. "Hits" on targets only count if the target actually falls down. As with BPCR, the shooter engages steel chickens, pigs, turkeys and rams, but they are scaled down for the distances. In this sport, a "chicken" measures a scant three inches by four inches and is shot at a distance of twenty-five yards! Doesn't sound hard? The image below measures about the size of an IHMSA chicken target. Set this seventy-five feet away and think about trying to hit five of them.

Shooters shoot at five of each target per round. A maximum score is 40 points. "Ties" are usually broken by setting up chicken targets on the hundred-yard line for a "shoot off." It's an impressive sight to see.

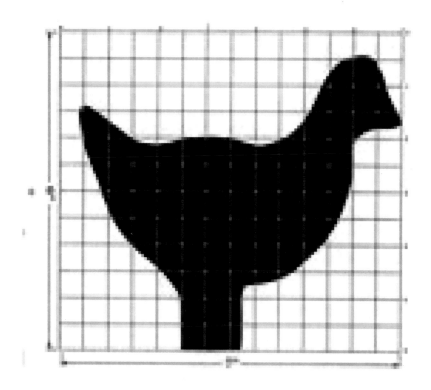

Sample "chicken" target from BPCR.NET website sized for IHMSA

For more information on IHMSA, check out http://www.ihmsa.com/.

Shotgun Games

Most shotgun games mimic hunting or strive to improve the participant's hunting skills. This makes shotgun sports wildly popular with hunters and others who seek the challenge of hitting fast-moving aerial targets. The three most popular shotgun games are trap, skeet, and sporting clays. This section takes a look at each and briefly outlines the sport.

Shotgun facilities at the Cherokee Gun Club, Gainesville, Georgia

TRAP

Trap is one of the oldest shotgun games and traces its roots back to the late 1700s. In fact many of the terms used in shotgun sports today hearken back to the early evolution of trap. In the early days, trap was a sport for gentlemen (read: rich). In those days, they didn't use clay or pitch targets . . . they used real birds (usually passenger pigeons). The bird was either caged or was "trapped" under the manservant's (or "trapper") top hat. A string was then attached to the hat or trap. The gentleman then yelled "pull" to signal the man to pull the string on the trap. A hit on a target is scored as "dead," and a miss is scored as "lost" because the bird would fly away, never to return! So the terms "trap," "dead," "lost," and "bird" as well as the command "pull" all go back to the 1700s. The last record of using "live" birds in a trap competition dates back to the 1920s when the practice was stopped (most likely due to the extinction of passenger pigeons)!

There are several variations to the game of trap. These are American trap, Wobble trap, Olympic trap, Double trap, and Nordic trap. On the whole, all forms of trap lie in the speed that the bird is thrown and the way the targets are presented to the shooter.

Trap shooters

The most popular forms of trap in North America are American and Wobble trap.

In these games, five shooters stand in a semicircle behind the bunker (where the clay thrower is located). Each fires one at a time in sequence. Shooters shoot five "birds" each at a station then rotate to the next position. A "round" of trap is then, twenty-five shots. Typically, four rounds are shot in a match. Often there will be a twenty-five round "shoot off" for the top-scoring competitors to break any ties (and for bragging rights). Wobble trap is similar to American trap but differs in the type of target machine. The Wobble trap machine alternates left to right and in angle to make the presentation of the target much more challenging to the shooter.

Trap field – shooter positions marked with "T"

For more information, check out the Amateur Trap Association's website at www1.shootata.com.

SKEET

Skeet is an exciting sport that epitomizes hand-eye coordination. The word "skeet" comes from the Scandinavian word for "shoot." The game was developed in the early to mid 1920s, as a fun way to practice "wing shooting." "Wing shooting" means shooting aerial targets that are crossing in front of the shooter. Since the targets are moving "sideways" relative to the shooter, the shooter must aim in front of the target. This is called "lead-ing" the target. Unlike trap, where targets are thrown from the center of the field, out away from the shooters; in skeet, the targets are thrown from the sides, across the shooter. Shooters still form a semicircle around the field and move from position to position, but there are eight positions (instead of five like in trap). Another important difference in skeet is that shooter generally participate using four different shotgun gauges: 12, 20, 28 and .410 gauges. Many have a single shotgun with multiple barrel sets, or "sleeves" that screw into their existing barrels that reduce the inside diameter of the bore.

Like trap, the early skeet shooters tended to be well-off. This changed during World War II. The U.S. government discovered that shooting at inexpensive clay targets with inexpensive shotgun ammunition was a ter-rific way to train gunners to shoot down airplanes! As a result, a whole new breed of shooter was created that spanned all economic strata. And this continues to this day.

Also like trap shooters move around the spokes of the semicircle. The throwers are located in two buildings on either side of the field. These buildings are referred to as "houses." The left side house is a two-story affair and throws a high, crossing target. This is known as the "high house". The building on the right side of the field throws a target that crosses the shooter at an upward angle. This is known as the "low house."

Skeet Field - Shooter Positions are marked with "S"

Skeet field showing the detail of the "High House"

For more information, check out the National Skeet Shooting Association (NSSA) website at www.mynssa.com.

SPORTING CLAYS

The game of "sporting clays" is often called "Golf with Guns." Just as a golfer follows a "course" that has specific holes to maneuver, the sporting clays shooter navigates a course. The parallels don't stop there. Just as a golfer must avoid obstacles such as sand traps, water hazards, and the "rough," sporting clays shooters must be mindful of trees blocking their shots. The sporting clays shooter has a "menu" of how many shots to fire at each station. This is roughly equivalent to "par" for a golfer.

The modern sporting clays facility is set up with at least fourteen stations. Each station challenges the shooter by varying the target presentation. In some cases, the shooter calls for the target (by yelling "pull") and can't see the thrower! Unlike trap and skeet, the shooter doesn't always shoot at the same-sized target. There are ½-sized targets ("springing teal"), and extra thick heavy targets (called "rabbits") that skip across the ground. It is not uncommon for a "menu" to contain multiple target presentations such as a fast crossing target followed by a low, fast rabbit. Very challenging, and *very* fun.

Often, to save space, a single facility will be set up with multiple throwers. These facilities are typically called "five stands" because they contain five shooting stations (like a trap field).

Five stand sporting clays setup at Prairie Sands Nebraska

Epilogue

OK, THAT'S IT. YOU'RE NOW PREPARED TO GO OUT AND start looking at and shooting guns. I encourage you all to go to a gun range and rent a gun (or fire the guns you have). Whatever you might decide, I want to encourage you to do it safely!

Photo Credits

1. http://detonicsusa.com/firearms/911011_sm.gif, September 11, 2006
2. www.lawtonpd.com/images/glock.jpg, September 13, 2006
3. www.midsouthshooterssupply.com/contenderg2.asp, September 13, 2006
4. www.cobrapistols.com/images/derringer_standard.gif, September 13, 2006
5. www.rpgfirearms.com.au/HI%20RES/HAMMERLI%20SP20.jpg, September 13, 2006
6. www.emf-company.com/images3/1860-henry-rifle-blue-24.jpg, September 13, 2006
7. www.emf-company.com/images3/1866-rifle-20.jpg, September 13, 2006
8. www.emf-company.com/images3/1873-lever-action-rifle.jpg, September 13, 2006
9. http://upload.wikimedia.org/wikipedia/commons/4/47/Sturmgewehr_44.jpg, September 13, 2006
10. www.remingtonle.com/images/rifles/m7615d.jpg, September 13, 2006
11. www.cz-usa.com/data/productimg/main062.png, September 13, 2006
12. www.coyotecap.com/images/99old10001.jpg, September 13, 2006
13. www.ar15.biz/images/norinco_982.jpg, September 13, 2006
14. www.mossberg.com/images/products/500/54282.jpg, September 13, 2006
15. www.charlesdaly.com/images/firearms/shotguns/semi-auto/large/Field%20Semi-Auto%20Advantage%20Timber%20HD.jpg, September 13, 2006
16. www.ruger-firearms.com/Firearms/images/Products/06L.jpg, September 13, 2006

17. http://www.texasranger.org/dispatch/11/ Graphics/87WinchesterOverall.gif, September 13, 2006

18. Available, http://www.hipowersandhandguns.com/Image34.jpg, September 13, 2006

19. Available, http://www.speer-bullets.com/images/Bullets/ cartridge/1044.jpg, September 13, 2006

20. Available, http://www.mortonbooth.com/images/940 index.jpg, September 13, 2006

21. http://us.st11.yimg.com/us.st.yimg.com/I/sarsam_1915_117698193, September 13, 2006

22. Available, http://www.ftknox.com/gun-safe-images/prot-fire-gun-safe519.jpg, September 13, 2006

23. http://www.sentrysafe.com/images/Products/A3860.jpg, September 13, 2006

24. http://gunvault.com/nss-folder/pictures/safes.jpg, September 13, 2006

25. Available, http://www.triggerlock.com/clublocks.jpg, September 13, 2006

26. http://www.midwayusa.com/mediasvr.dll/ highresimage?saleitemid=453246, September 13, 2006

27. http://www.gunaccessories.com/Hoppes/FamousNo9Bottle.jpg, September 13, 2006

28. https://www.pagerpal.com/images/pager.jpg, September 13, 2006

29. http://69.94.104.142/media/duty_gear_images/gal-mc.jpg, September 13, 2006

30. http://img224.imageshack.us/img224/9773/fieldstrip17yo0.jpg, September 13, 2006

31. http://www.oakwoodsportsmanslodge.com/images/osl14.jpg, September 13, 2006

32. http://www.cherokeeipsc.org/pictures/January05_2005/cherokee%20 jan05%20022a.jpg, September 13, 2006

33. http://www.prairiesands.com/photos/gallery/Shoot6.JPG, September 13, 2006

Index